# Bright Ideas Writing

Written by David Wray

Published by Scholastic Publications Ltd,
Marlborough House, Holly Walk,
Leamington Spa, Warwickshire CV32 4LS.

**Reprinted 1987, 1988.**

Some ideas drawn from Scholastic
magazines.

Written by David Wray
Edited by Jane Bishop
Illustrations by Jane Bottomley

Printed in Great Britain by
Loxley Brothers Ltd, Sheffield

ISBN 0 590 707019

Front and back cover: Martyn Chillmaid
Thanks to Lakey Lane Primary School, Birmingham for
supplying material for cover.

# Contents

# Introduction

The recent remarkable growth of interest in the teaching of writing has not simply expanded the ideas we have about children's writing; it has also changed them in far-reaching ways. Previously the so-called 'creative' writing movement had implied that all that was needed was to stimulate children and, assuming they had mastered the basic mechanics of writing, they would develop their abilities simply by doing it. We now realise this was naive, and that we need to concentrate on what children are doing when they write.

The focus, then, has moved from stimulus for writing, to the process itself. Although the ideas in this book include some stimulus points for writing, they concentrate much more on ways of assisting the process. These include ideas for making writing meaningful and purposeful for children, and also for developing and extending revision and writing for a specific audience. Ideas are also given for ways of harnessing new technology, in particular word processors, to the development of writing.

Guidelines are given for each activity about the size of group and the intended age-range. These are, however, not intended to be interpreted rigidly.

## FORMING A LITERARY ENVIRONMENT

For children to see writing as meaningful, they have to become aware that it is important, and indeed essential, in the world outside school. There is a tendency for them to perceive writing as an exclusively school activity. The purpose of many of the ideas in this section is to demonstrate the opposite. Children can be introduced to the wide range of ways writing is used in the world, the many forms it takes and of the purposes it serves. They can also be shown that even adults, including their teachers, have to think about writing when attempting to express ideas in the best way. There are also suggestions here for ways of presenting children's writing to others, thereby ensuring that it is read and valued.

## PRE-WRITING

Children's initial experiences of the writing process are often hampered by their lack of command of the technical skills of producing words on the page. The suggestions in this section have two aims. Firstly, they give ideas for how to give children experience of composition without them being held back by the problem of handwriting and, secondly, they suggest ways of ensuring that early handwriting training is such that it makes growth of writing skill easy.

## PROCESSES OF WRITING

This section deals with the place of revision in the writing process. Many of the ideas stress the benefits to be gained from collaboration in writing, whether between children, or between teacher and child. The idea of the 'writing conference', a term coined by Donald Graves, is central to this collaboration. Perhaps even more important, however, is the concept underlying these ideas – that writing should no longer be seen as a form of test for children. Instead the children can learn to improve their writing, and to enlist the help of others whilst doing so.

## WRITING FOR A PURPOSE

Adults never write without a clearly defined purpose. Children, however, very often write only for their teacher's eyes, after which their work is not read in a real sense, but marked, which implies a quite different approach. This section looks at ways of extending the purposes for which children write. Gradually they will come to appreciate the differing demands of different audiences for their writing, and how to structure it accordingly.

The ideas here, naturally, demand a certain level of ability in writing from the children. Consequently most of them specify a minimum age of six years. These activities can, however, be done with even younger children if the burden of writing is taken away from them, ie the teacher does the writing for them.

## TYPES OF WRITING

This section consists of ideas for getting children writing, and includes suggestions for developing a wide variety of types of writing. Writing stories, that is, in a narrative form, is important and natural for children, and there are some suggestions for it here. Other types of writing are also given attention: poetry, descriptive writing, and the often-neglected use of writing to communicate information and to persuade. This section makes no attempt to be comprehensive; there are many other sources of suggestions for writing stimulus points. Its main purpose is to suggest the need for balance in a child's writing experience.

## TECHNICAL SKILLS OF WRITING

This book stresses the process of composition, but that does not imply that the ability to transcribe accurately what one composes is unimportant. It is vital, but it is also necessary to ensure that transcription skills are taught meaningfully. The ability to spell accurately and to punctuate correctly are important in writing, but they are not the only, or even the most important things. In the adult world what people write tends to be judged more on what they have to say. The ideas here have to be seen in this light. The majority of them concern ways of handling spelling, a familiar management problem for most primary teachers.

## USING NEW TECHNOLOGIES

Computers have had an impact on most aspects of the primary school curriculum, but perhaps their most significant effect has been, or will be, in the area of writing. The word processor can revolutionise children's approach to writing, as it almost forces them to revise and re-revise what they write. Children seem to take to it very readily, and rapidly learn to use it. At first they appreciate the fact that the word processor allows them to make mistakes which can easily be corrected. Children quickly learn that because of this, they can concentrate first of all on what they want to say, leaving attention to technical things like spellings until later. Also, they quickly see it as a labour-saving device. They may be encouraged to draft and revise their writing without using the word processor, but the problem with this is, of course, the amount of writing and re-writing which is involved. Children can be put off revising their work because of this 'copying it out again'. The word processor avoids this difficulty because alterations can be easily made on the screen before the writing is finally committed to paper.

This section contains ideas for using this extremely valuable tool, as well as others for putting computers to effective use in developing writing.

David Wray

# Forming a literary environment

# The literate home corner

### Age range
Four to seven.

### Group size
Individuals or small groups (four or five children).

### What you need
A home corner equipped with the usual domestic items. A supply of materials to provide a literacy dimension, eg pens, pencils, paper, telephone directories, newspapers, magazines, cookery books, advertising leaflets etc.

### What to do
Encourage children playing in the home corner to include literacy activities in their play. Ask them to do what their parents do at home, and provide the requisite materials. Things to do include writing letters to friends, filling in forms, writing and reading recipes, writing shopping lists, writing down telephone numbers of friends and doing crosswords. Include activities which involve mostly reading such as reading magazines, looking up programmes in the TV guide and using telephone directories.

### Follow-up
Some children might be able to go on to produce their own written materials to practise reading on. For example, they could compile their own class telephone directories, their own versions of TV schedules or their own newspapers and magazines.

# A scribble corner

### Age range
Four to six.

### Group size
Individuals or small groups (four or five children).

### What you need
A place in the classroom where individual children can work undisturbed. A variety of writing implements and surfaces, erasers, rulers, cards, charts, posters with models of writing on them.

### What to do
Give children opportunities to practise scribbling and 'writing' (even if only 'pretend' writing) whenever the chance arises. They need to experiment with a variety of writing tools including pencils, crayons, pens, charcoal, both thick and thin wax crayons, and on a variety of writing surfaces such as paper and card of various thicknesses and colours. Do not direct them too much but tell them that the corner is for practising writing. If there are models of writing around for them to look at, they will begin to pick up some important messages about writing, ie that it goes in lines across the page, that it uses letters and words that they may be familiar with from other places, and, if they are encouraged to 'read' their writing to someone (even if they have to make it up), that writing is about passing on messages.

### Follow-up
Gradually the scribble corner will turn into a writing corner as the children become more skilled at producing writing which conveys a message. Their writing efforts need to be dealt with positively and displayed in the scribble/writing corner either on the walls or in home-made books.

### Cautionary note
Beware of using tracing paper in the scribble corner. When children are tracing writing unsupervised it is easy for them to get into bad handwriting habits. Teach letter formation alongside the use of the scribble corner; it is important that the children do not 'unlearn' the lessons they learn about handwriting.

# The writing corner

### Age range
Six to eleven.

### Group size
Individuals or small groups (four or five children).

### What you need
A corner of the room with a couple of tables and chairs, and a supply of paper, unlined and lined, various pens, pencils, erasers, rulers, liquid paper and a typewriter if possible.

### What to do
Set up a writing corner in the same way as you will probably have a reading corner. The corner should ideally be available to children to use at any time they feel they have something they want to write. Equip it with the tools they need for writing and arrange it so that it stimulates them to write. Display lots of examples of writing, both story and information books, as well as writing produced by the children themselves. Children using the corner should be free to write about whatever they wish, but it will stimulate many of them if you display interesting pictures, posters, word collections etc as starting points. These will need to be changed regularly.

### Follow-up
Let the children know you value the writing they do in the writing corner. This can be done by you or the children reading out pieces of writing to the class during sharing times, or by displaying writing on the wall or in class anthologies. Occasionally a piece of writing done by one child may inspire others to write about a similar theme. These pieces can be displayed alongside pictures, posters etc relevant to the theme.

# A writing trail

## Age range
Seven to eleven.

## Group size
No larger than ten to twelve children.

## What you need
Clipboards for each child, a camera if possible.

## What to do
In the same way as you might take a group of children on a nature trail, take them on a writing trail around your local streets. Get them to note down, and preferably photograph, examples of the writing they will see around them as they walk. As they note down what they see, ask them to think about why that writing is there, who is intended to read it, and anything distinctive about the way in which it is written. If it is not possible to photograph the examples, ask them to copy them down. The trail will probably not need to be very long because the children will soon be overwhelmed with examples. Back in school an analysis can be made of the types of writing found, their purposes, and intended audiences, and the results displayed alongside copied examples or photographs.

## Follow-up
The examples of environmental print collected can be used as a starting point for the following idea.

10

# Modelling types of writing

## Age range
Seven to eleven.

## Group size
Whole class or groups of six or more children.

## What you need
Examples of a variety of writing styles, eg instruction leaflets, notices, advertisements, letters, recipes and poems.

## What to do
Discuss with the children the various styles of writing. Encourage them to think about why each piece of writing was written, who it was aimed at, and what is special about the way it is written. After a lot of discussion the children can go on to try to produce their own versions of one or more of these types of writing. (See chapter on Types of writing, page 58, for ideas for making this purposeful.)

## Follow-up
A collection of examples of writing from the everyday world can be made. This 'environmental' writing can be displayed as 'Writing around us', alongside children's analyses of what is special about the various types, plus their own attempts at producing it.

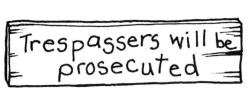

# A celebration of writing

## Age range
Six to eleven.

## Group size
Whole class.

## What you need
Examples of different kinds of writing including various pieces of children's writing, writing in different languages and type styles. (See pages 122–124).

## What to do
Mount a display of as many different varieties of writing as possible. Children could research and write pieces for the display in a whole range of languages, including Punjabi, Gujerati, Greek, French etc. This could perhaps be displayed around a common theme, eg different ways of saying 'Good Morning', or 'Happy New Year'.

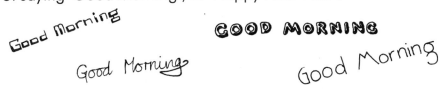

   You could also mount a display of different typestyles, and styles of handwriting, either provided by yourself or by the children. Invite people who write in different ways to come to demonstrate to the class. You could probably find someone who was taught to write in copperplate style, or italics, and you may be lucky enough to have parents or children who can write Chinese or Arabic. This small project on writing could last a week or more as you collect and discuss hand and typewriting styles.

# Teacher as writer 1

### Age range
Six to eleven.

### Group size
Small groups (six to eight children) or whole class.

### What you need
A good stimulus point for both you and the children to write about.

### What to do
Instead of the children writing their stories alone tell them you are going to write a story as well. Don't think about it too much beforehand so that you are in the same position as the children when you begin to write. While you are writing, occasionally look in the dictionary or the thesaurus for a word, or go and ask a child if he/she can help you with a word or another point in your writing. Share your efforts with the children when you have finished and show them your writing. Do not make it specially neat and tidy, but show them that you often change your mind when you are writing and cross things out, re-order and add new ideas. Talk to them about any points at which you got stuck during your writing and ask them what you could have done. Finally, ask for their opinion of your writing; be prepared for it to be critical.

This activity can be somewhat nerve-wracking, and you will undoubtedly feel very exposed by it. If you do it often enough you *will* get used to it, and it will certainly help you to understand the experience of the children.

### Follow-up
Make this a regular activity. Occasionally bring in pieces of writing you have started at home, ask the children's advice and show them that asking others' for help can be worthwhile.

# Teacher as writer 2

**Age range**
Six to eleven.

**Group size**
Whole class.

**What you need**
An overhead projector with a blank acetate sheet and appropriate pens. If these are not available the activity could be done using large sheets of paper fastened to an easel.

**What to do**
Tell the children that you are going to write something with their help. Choose a subject matter which interests you but do not pre-plan what to write. Write as you think aloud on the overhead projector or easel. Stop frequently as you get stuck with particular words or ideas. Ask for advice from the children and encourage discussion about how you should express yourself. Demonstrate that writing is not a flowing process but is, in fact, very jerky and full of stops and starts. Show also that you are prepared to alter and rearrange what you have written.

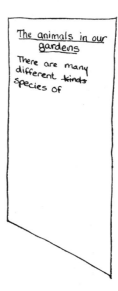

**Follow-up**
This idea can be developed into a regular activity for collaborative story-writing either with a group or the whole class. The teacher, or a sufficiently fast-writing child can act as scribe while the rest of the group decide on the direction the writing will take and on its content.

13

# A literature environment

### Age range
Four to eleven.

### Group size
Whole class.

### What you need
Lots of examples of literature in all forms at various levels.

### What to do
Children's writing will obviously improve in quality the more access they are given to good quality writing. They should always be surrounded by good literature. Have displays of children's story and information books and children's poetry which are regularly changed, and which are commented upon and brought to the children's attention. Encourage children to read as much as possible, and read to them too. Children who are able to write can be encouraged to write stories, poems etc like those they have read. 'Can you write me a story of your own about *My Naughty Little Sister*? Can you write me another verse to *The Jumblies*?'

Older children will be able to begin discussions about particular styles of writing. They can think about what makes informative writing different from narrative writing, and some of them will be able to go on to discuss what makes different authors' writing distinctive, eg 'How can you tell this is a poem by Eleanor Farjeon and not Michael Rosen?' Encourage children to talk, not just about what they read, but also about the way in which it is written.

### Follow-up
Some children will be able to go on to write in similar styles to particular authors. Michael Rosen's poetry is not too difficult to imitate, and several children will be able to begin a story in the same way as Ted Hughes begins *The Iron Man*.

# Scrolls

### Age range
Six to eleven.

### Group size
Whole class.

### What you need
Some means of heating and/or slightly burning paper, ribbon, red wax.

### What to do
Some of the writing children do can be made into scroll books, which is how books were produced a long time ago. Children may have seen treasure maps like this, or be familiar with the way the Romans used to produce books. When they have written their stories onto pieces of paper, roll them up. Tie them with ribbon, and seal with wax. Use a coin as an imprint for the seal. They may also be baked in an oven for about ten minutes which will make them brown, brittle and ancient-looking. If the edges are singed this will also make them look old and battered.

# Address books

## Age range
Seven to eleven.

## Group size
Individuals.

## What you need
Small-sized exercise books.

## What to do
Children can make their own address or telephone books to hold details of their friends and classmates. The first step is to decide how many pages to allot to each letter of the alphabet. If the books they are using are big enough, the simplest solution is to allow one page per letter, but if not, then it is usual to combine the less common letters such as XYZ. If the children can manage it, it is nice to cut the right hand edge of the book so that they can turn instantly to the correct page. This needs careful working out and cutting, but is intriguing for children. A similar technique might be adopted for their spelling books.

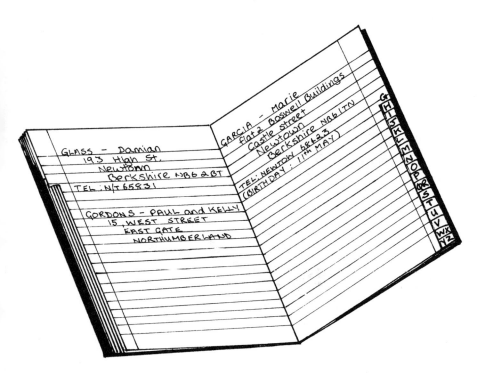

## Follow-up
Compiling address books gives scope for teaching the correct way to set out addresses, and provides a great deal of practice at doing this.

# Biographies

## Age range
Six to eleven.

## Group size
Individuals.

## What you need
Scrapbooks, either bought or made by the children.

## What to do
Children can combine writing with photographs and pictures to make scrapbooks which tell the story of their lives, or the lives of their friends/brothers/sisters/parents etc. This will involve a good deal of research, asking questions and interviewing. They will need to find a quick way of recording the information they collect before reworking it into a biography. They will need to discuss the best way of presenting their books, and of interspersing factual information with humorous stories, and fitting in the illustrations. They will also need to write captions for the pictures and photos.

## Follow-up
Scrapbooks can be a useful way of collecting and presenting children's writing. If the children are shown how to make them, they will be able to produce them to order to fit particular projects. They might collect pictures, press cuttings and pieces of their own writing about their favourite film star/footballer/pop star etc, and once they have decided how best to present the information, make a scrapbook.

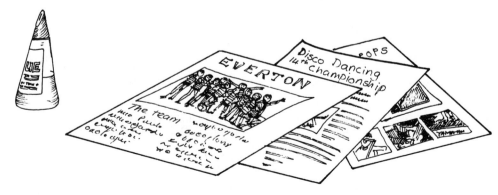

# Getting into publication

**Age range**
Six to eleven.

**Group size**
Whole class.

**What you need**
No special requirements, although a typewriter or word processor would be a real asset.

**What to do**
Make it a regular feature in your classroom to publish children's writing. Not every piece of writing can be used, but aim for every child to have his/her writing published at least once a fortnight. Preferably the writing should be typed or printed via the computer, but if these means are not available most children will be willing to write out their work neatly if they know it is going to be published. The writing could then go either into a large class book, perhaps on a particular topic, or into a child's individual book. This individual book could be a cumulative collection of the child's writing, or could contain just one piece. Try the latter at least a few times. Every child will be thrilled with the idea that he/she has written a book. Books can be displayed in the classroom, and can also be borrowed and read by other children.

# Binding your own books 1

**Age range**
Seven to eleven.

**Group size**
Individuals or groups of four to six.

**What you need**
Paper and cardboard.

**What to do**
To make simple booklets of no more than 12 pages, the first step is to decide on the shape the booklet will be. You might make long narrow books about trains, tall thin books about lighthouses, or, more adventurously, books shaped like their subject.

Having worked out how many pages your book will need, fold each sheet of paper carefully in half. Press the fold to make a sharp crease. Some of the pages could be of a different colour or texture to the rest.

Stack the sheets together, with the folds in the middle, see figure 1.

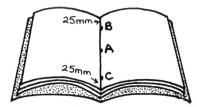

Figure 1

Make the cover out of card, slightly bigger than the pages all the way round. Score the fold.

Use a large darning needle with a sharp point and strong white thread at least twice the length of the spine of the book. Do not knot the ends of the thread.

Open your book at the centre and make three marks on the crease, one in the middle at A, and the other two, at B and C, 25 mm from the top and bottom. Include the cover at the bottom of the pile of pages, figure 2.

Figure 2

Use the needle to make holes through all the pages at A, B and C. Make sure the pages do not move about while you do this.

To sew, hold the pages firmly so that the holes stay in line. Push the needle with the thread through the middle hole, A, from the inside. Make sure that the end of the thread is left inside, figure 3.

From the outside push the needle through the top hole, B, and take it down the inside to the bottom hole, C, figure 4.

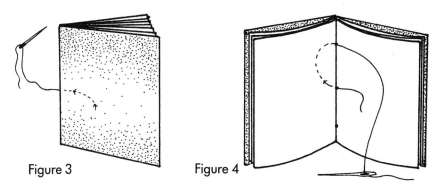

Figure 3      Figure 4

Push it through the bottom hole, C, to the outside again, figure 5.

Bring the needle back to the inside through the middle hole, A, figure 6.

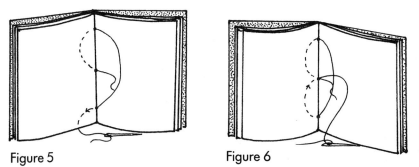

Figure 5      Figure 6

Unthread the needle. You now have two loose ends of thread hanging from the centre hole. Pull them tight, and place them on either side of the thread which runs down the fold. Tie a reef knot, making sure that it traps the centre thread, figure 7.

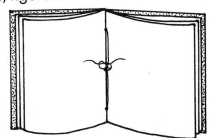

Figure 7

# Binding your own books 2

### Age range
Seven to eleven.

### Group size
Individuals or groups of four to six.

### What you need
Paper and cardboard.

### What to do
For bigger books, make one or more sets of sewn pages and join them together.

Cut a strip of paper 30 mm wide and the same length as the pages. Fold it in half down the middle. This will form a hinge between two adjoining sections of the book. Make as many as you require and glue them between each section, see figure 1.

Next, close the pages and compress them with a heavy book placed on top. Measure the thickness of the book at the folded edge. This measurement will be the width of the spine of the cover. If you are making your book from two or more sets of pages, bind them together with brown sticky tape, figure 2.

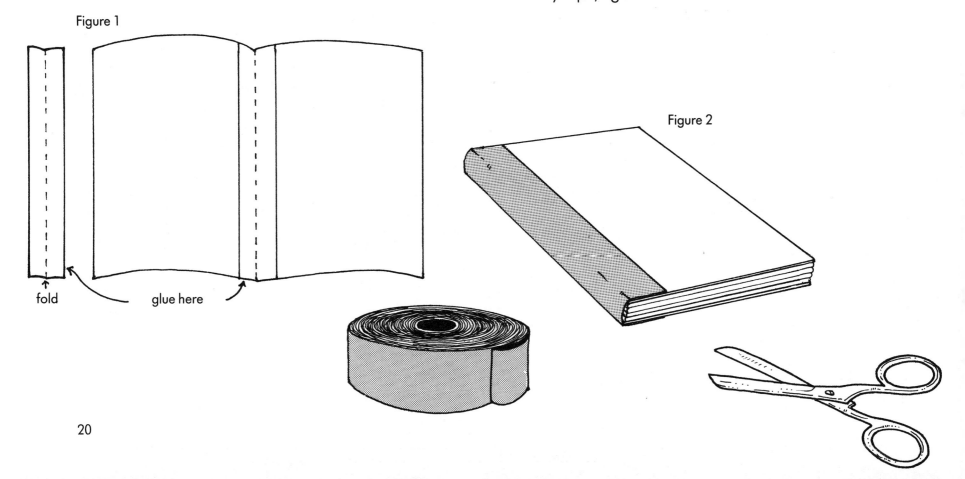

Figure 1

fold

glue here

Figure 2

# Covering your own books

### Age range
Seven to eleven.

### Group size
Individuals or groups of four to six.

### What you need
Paper and cardboard.

### What to do
Covers are best made separately and glued to the card cover of your prepared book. For a simple booklet, make a more elaborate cover out of two pieces of card, one for the front and one for the back, so that, when they are glued on, there is a slight gap down the fold. This will make the book easier to open, see figure 1.

For the thicker book with a spine, cut out three pieces of card, one for the front cover, one for the back and one for the spine, figure 2.

A cloth-bound book looks expensive; preferably use a plain-coloured light material. Paper that is textured looks effective, as does paper which you have previously decorated by marbling or with wax resist designs.

Make sure the paper or cloth is at least 20 or 30 mm larger all round than the cover. Glue the cover cards and spine onto the paper or cloth, leaving a small (1–2 mm) gap between each card, figure 3. Use Polycell adhesive or watered-down PVA. Rub all the edges with a ruler to ensure a neat finish. Turn the cover over and glue down all the flaps, figure 4. When it is dry, use a spray or stick adhesive to glue the last page of the book to the inside of the back cover. Then glue the spine. Finally, glue the first page of the book to the inside of the front cover. Leave it under pressure to dry.

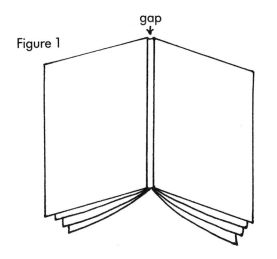

Figure 1

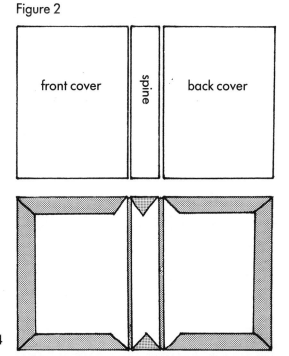

Figure 2

Figure 4

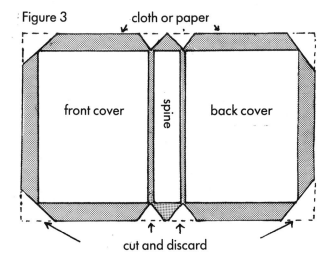

Figure 3

# Pre-writing

# Using drawing to begin writing

### Age range
Four to six.

### Group size
From individuals to whole classes.

### What you need
Drawing instruments such as wax crayons, felt tips.

### What to do
Children will readily draw pictures. While they are drawing, they can pick up lots of skills which will help them when they come to learn to write. Show them the way to hold their crayons; they will later learn to hold pencils and pens in the same way. Encourage them to concentrate on what they are drawing for increasingly longer periods of time. Get them to talk about what they have drawn, and, most important, what they are going to draw next. Asking for a commentary on their drawing can lead them to be more reflective about it. Encourage them to come back to their drawings after a few hours, or perhaps even a day or two, to alter things, or add more fine details.

### Follow-up
Later children can be asked to actually tell stories through drawings. Talk about beginnings, middles and ends, and encourage children to draw stories with these features, either in one drawing, or by a series of drawings.

# Scribble writing

### Age range
Four to six.

### Group size
Individuals.

### What you need
No special requirements.

### What to do
From children's very first days in school they can be encouraged to 'write', that is, to pass on messages through making marks on paper. Most children will have an idea of what writing involves, and many of them will be quite familiar with what it looks like. Ask them to write things for you and for other people in the school. These efforts may be nothing more than scribble, but praise them for ways in which it resembles 'real' writing, eg goes in lines, starts in the correct place, looks like letters etc.

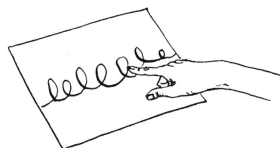

### Follow-up
Ask children to read back what they have 'written'. Encourage them by putting your finger on the place where they should start, and by responding to what they say.

# Captioning drawings 1

### Age range
Four to six.

### Group size
Individuals.

### What you need
No special requirements.

### What to do
When children have done a drawing or painting you can ask them for a sentence or caption to accompany it. Write this underneath the drawing. Read the caption aloud as you write it. Make sure the children are aware that you are actually writing what they said. You can stress this by making it explicit, eg 'And now I'm writing "Mummy"; look, "Mum – my". Can you say that?' Get the children to read the caption back to you, or with you as you point to the words. They can then trace over your writing. Help them by pointing out where their pencil should start, and in which way they should form the letters. Say each word as they finish it and get them to repeat it after you.

### Follow-up
Later children will be able to trace your captions without any help. Keep this activity under close observation, however. It is very easy for children to pick up bad letter-formation habits through tracing, which can be difficult to eradicate later.

# Captioning drawings 2

**Age range**
Four to six.

**Group size**
Individuals.

**What you need**
No special requirements.

**What to do**
When children can trace your captions fairly competently the next stage is that of copy-writing. Leave space underneath the caption for them to copy what you have written. At first you may want to give them some help by writing the caption again in dotted letters, which they can then join up. You can then omit this step and let them copy the caption themselves. Again keep a close eye on them for the first few times they do this, to avoid letter-formation problems. Get them to bring their work to you when they have finished so that they can read out what they have written.

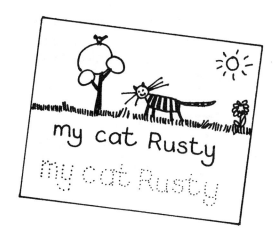

# Captioning drawings 3

**Age range**
Four to six.

**Group size**
Individuals.

**What you need**
No special requirements.

**What to do**
Eventually children will be capable of writing their own captions for their drawings. This stage is the beginning of 'free' writing. It has the benefit that children have a chance to rehearse through drawing what they want to write before actually writing. Get them to talk about their drawing, and help them decide what they will write. At first you will need to sit with them while they are writing their caption, and give whatever help is necessary, but try to encourage independence from the beginning. This will help avoid some problems later. For example, if they ask you how they can write a particular word, encourage them from the start to consult the word bank, or word lists. Do this with them, thus demonstrating the procedure you want them to adopt when later they write by themselves.

# Beginning composition 1

## Age range
Four to seven.

## Group size
Individuals.

## What you need
Magnet boards with magnetic figures, felt boards with figures, or simple cardboard cut-out figures.

## What to do
Children can begin to learn about story composition without efficient handwriting skills. Get them to use aids such as cardboard figures to illustrate stories as they tell them, either to themselves or to other listeners. Encourage them to remember the stories they tell and to tell them again to other people, perhaps changing them a little to improve them. Get them to comment on their stories, and to ask their listeners for comments.

This idea can also work using toys as a vehicle for story-telling.

## Follow-up
Children may be able to tell their stories into a tape recorder. These recordings can be listened to by other children, as the author illustrates them with the cut-out figures. Again encourage comments, which may lead to modifications to the stories.

# Beginning composition 2

## Age range
Four to seven.

## Group size
Individuals.

## What you need
Sets of puppets, which could be made by the children themselves.

## What to do
Children can act out a play with puppets. This can either be from a story which they have heard, or a story they have made up. Talk with them about what will happen in the play and get them, as far as possible, to anticipate the plot. When they have performed the play, talk with them about what happened, and ask them if they can do it again, perhaps changing it a little. Encourage reworking of the same idea. Again this activity gives children experience in composing without the limitation of writing.

## Follow-up
An excellent way of following this up would be to video record the puppet play. This could then be played back to the whole class, and they could be asked for their suggestions for modifications.

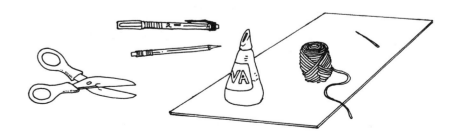

# Beginning composition 3

### Age range
Four to seven.

### Group size
Individuals or groups of three to four children.

### What you need
Several sets of three or four pictures which tell stories. These can be cut from magazines, from young children's comics or drawn by the teacher.

### What to do
Get the children to talk about the pictures and to try to arrange them in order to tell a story. When they have done this they can then tell the story they have made. Encourage them to go back to the same pictures a little later, and see if they can remember the story they told. Encourage elaboration and modification of their stories.

### Follow-up
They can, as with all activities involving spoken stories, tell their stories into the tape recorder, for later use with other children and by themselves.

# Beginning composition 4

**Age range**
Four to seven.

**Group size**
Whole class or fairly large groups.

**What you need**
A story which interests the class.

**What to do**
After telling the class the story, talk about which parts they liked best. Individuals or small groups could be told to draw pictures of parts of the story. When these are completed, discuss the whole story with the class to work out the order the parts should go in. The pictures can then be made into a class book of the story. Each picture needs a caption to explain its part in the story. These can be discussed with the class and read with them. If they are able, some children can write the captions themselves, either copying, or tracing the teacher's writing.

# Dictated stories

## Age range
Three to six.

## Group size
Individuals.

## What you need
A typewriter would be excellent, although it is possible to do without.

## What to do
During free-choice or playtime activities in nursery/reception classes, one of the things you could do is place yourself in the writing corner, with a typewriter, or, if this is not possible, a 'grown-up' pen. Encourage children to come and tell you things which you then type out, or write down. Read the messages out for the children, and encourage them to try to read them back, even if they make up what is there. They can then take away their 'stories', and tell other people about them.

# Ready to write?

## Age range
Four to six.

## Group size
Individuals.

## What you need
Something for the children to draw with which makes a clear line, eg a soft black pencil, a large fibre pen.

## What to do
Ask the children to draw a picture of themselves engaged in an action. Tell the children you want them to tell you a simple story, such as them kicking a ball, or chasing a friend. Do not encourage them to move on from their stage of drawing; if they are still at the scribbling stage, then accept that. Use the drawings to judge whether the children are ready to learn to make letters. They are probably ready when they can draw a person with details correctly placed, and can make one shape inside another.

not ready    almost ready    ready to write

## Follow-up
The activity of telling a simple story through drawing can in itself be enough to help children acquire sufficient motor control to be ready to form letters. If they are encouraged to communicate more, they will usually develop the means to do so.

# Teaching handwriting 1

**Age range**
Four to seven.

**Group size**
Individuals.

**What you need**
A variety of aids to teaching handwriting as described below.

**What to do**
Teach handwriting as a separate skill from story-writing. Teach it regularly and intensively, encouraging concentration and praising achievement. Provide children with a shallow sand or salt tray for practising letter formation, and begin by guiding their hands around the letters. Give them access to felt letters, sand-paper letters, wooden letters to trace round with their fingers. Be alert to them starting to trace in the correct place and proceeding in the correct direction (see copy sheets, pages 117–119).

Most publishers produce sheets of handwriting exercises and these can be used as long as they do not become a chore for the children. There are also computer programs available which draw selected letters slowly on the screen. Encourage children to follow the letters with their fingers as they are drawn, and then ask them to do it themselves on paper or in sand.

**Cautionary note**
Beware of too much copy-writing. If they are left to themselves to copy teacher's writing, young children can quickly pick up habits of movement which hinder them and which are hard to eradicate.

# Teaching handwriting 2

**Age range**
Four to seven.

**Group size**
Individuals.

**What you need**
No special requirements.

**What to do**
When first teaching handwriting to young children choose a script which will lead naturally to adult writing. Print script, as used in many initial reading schemes, is not helpful in this way. Print script letters are straight, and they are designed to stop abruptly on the line. Children then have to be re-educated to a flowing movement. If, instead, children are introduced from the beginning to a script with joining strokes at the base of the letters, which most five-year-olds should be able to master, their movements will be correct and joining up letters will take place almost automatically.

**Cautionary note**
Too much emphasis too soon on neatness inhibits the free-flowing movement which is essential to good, fast handwriting, as does too rigid an enforcement of a particular style.

# Teaching handwriting 3

**Age range**
Four to six.

**Group size**
Individuals.

**What you need**
Implements for writing with which the children feel comfortable.

**What to do**
In teaching the formation of letters, introduce letters in groups of similar kinds of movements. Letters such as

## adgq or rmnhk

will tend to be learnt more readily in this way. Do not use lined paper at the beginning of teaching letter formation. Children will tend to slow down if they have to concentrate on making their letters sit on the line. The aim should always be to get them into the habit of writing fairly quickly. Play games to encourage this, eg how many a's can you write in a minute? Once children have learnt the right way of forming a letter at speed, it is more difficult for them to do it wrongly.

**Follow-up**
The key to the efficient learning of handwriting is regular, fast writing practice. Use repetitive letter sequences such as 'gaga', or 'mimi', or funny words such as 'grr' or 'boo', which the children can enjoy writing without having to slow down and think about what they mean.

# The processes of writing

# Teaching revision 1

## Age range
Seven to eleven.

## Group size
Whole class.

## What you need
A story or other piece of writing written by a child.

## What to do
To introduce the idea of revising written work, use a piece of writing done by a child in the class. (Ask the child's permission for this first.) Read it out to the whole class. Stress how good it is already, but then ask the class if they can think of any ways in which it could be made even better. Make it a rule that if anybody offers criticisms they have to also say how it might be improved.

Begin by asking the class to think of things the writer might have added to the work: any extra events, any extra descriptions, any extra information needed. Then go on to ask them if anything should have been missed out. Later sessions like this can go on to think about sequence. Ask whether the writer has got everything in the right order, or whether the writing would have been better if things had been rearranged. Finally, the class's attention could be directed to the structure of the writing. Is there a good beginning, middle and end to the writing? If it is factual writing, is it introduced well? If it is a story, does it have an exciting beginning, and is the ending satisfying, or does it just tail off?

Clearly not all these things can be done in one session with one piece of writing. This kind of session could be a regular event over a period of months. Its purpose is to get the children used to the idea that writing is not entirely fixed as soon as it is written down for the first time, but can be changed and improved.

## Follow-up
After they have grasped the idea of revising in oral sessions, move on to using copies of the piece of writing, so that they can read it for themselves and see the effects of changes.

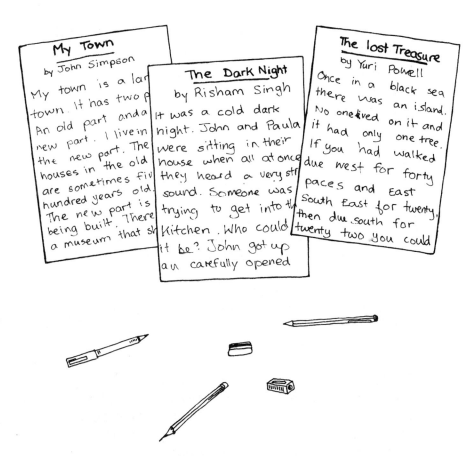

# Teaching revision 2

### Age range
Seven to eleven.

### Group size
Groups of four to six.

### What you need
Copies of stories written by children in the class.

### What to do
Give each group a copy of the same story to share. Tell them they are going to work together to:

- decide what is good about the story they have in front of them.
- decide whether they could suggest any ways it could be improved.

They could focus here on possible additions to the story, things they might leave out, possible changes in the order of events, descriptions etc, and ways the beginning or the ending might be improved.

Stress to the group that it is *not* their purpose at this time to criticise misspellings, mistakes in grammar or punctuation, or the writer's handwriting. It's probably a good idea to perfect these aspects on the copy before the group discuss it; perhaps by the story being typed out by an adult or very competent child.

### Follow-up
Later the group might let the original author of the writing know about their discussions. He or she would be free to take their advice and change the writing if he/she chooses, but would have the last word on changes.

# Teaching revision 3

### Age range
Seven to eleven.

### Group size
Whole class or groups of four upwards.

### What you need
Photocopies of original manuscripts of famous authors. Look in books on calligraphy, or in autobiographies of famous authors. If you cannot find one, then cheat and write one yourself!

### What to do
Explain that the manuscript you use was written by someone who was very famous for their writing, and very good at it. Ask the children for any comments they have. They will probably notice the handwriting (probably not very good, or even illegible), the spelling (if a piece from earlier than the nineteenth century is used this will be idiosyncratic) and the amount of crossings out. Ask them:

- how can someone with such bad handwriting, who is such a poor speller, be thought a good writer?
- why are there so many crossings out? Why could the author not get everything right first time? Relate the discussion to their own writing.

### Follow-up
Demonstrating that famous authors make mistakes and actually write messy work will be of little use in encouraging children to revise, if strict standards of accuracy and tidiness are subsequently applied to their first draft writing. Do not *make* them messy if they are not, but help them see when it is important to try their best with accuracy and tidiness, and when it is not so important.

35

# Collaborative editing

**Age range**
Seven to eleven.

**Group size**
From four to five children.

**What you need**
No special requirements.

**What to do**
Start children off writing stories individually in the usual way. Tell them that what they first write will be a first draft, and will be discussed and perhaps altered afterwards by groups of them. After they have all finished a first draft, arrange them into small groups and ask them to discuss and to try to improve each others, stories. Ask them to concentrate on:

- improvements to the content of the story;
- improvements to the sequence of the story;
- changes to any individual words;
- any other helpful remarks.

Stress that they are to be helpful about the stories they discuss. They are not allowed to find fault without suggesting ways of improving things. Make it clear that the original writer of the story can reject their suggestions if he/she wishes.

After this discussion, the original author can be allowed to rewrite the story.

**Follow-up**
This exercise will need to be done many times before the children really accept it and become good at doing it.

**Cautionary note**
Be careful about the composition of the groups for this activity. Think about how the children will react together. It is especially important not to put a very self-confident child together with a very shy child. You will need to ensure that all the children in the group are given a chance to express their ideas.

# Writing with revision in mind 1

**Age range**
Seven to eleven.

**Group size**
Individuals.

**What you need**
No special requirements.

**What to do**
When children are revising their own writing it is easy for things to get a bit messy. It can become difficult to see what changes they have actually made. To avoid some of the confusion this can cause, get them to write their early drafts on very broadly spaced lines, perhaps alternate lines, or even every third line. Then there will be space for alterations and additions to be made, without making the writing too messy to read.

# Writing with revision in mind 2

## Age range
Seven to eleven.

## Group size
Individuals.

## What you need
No special requirements.

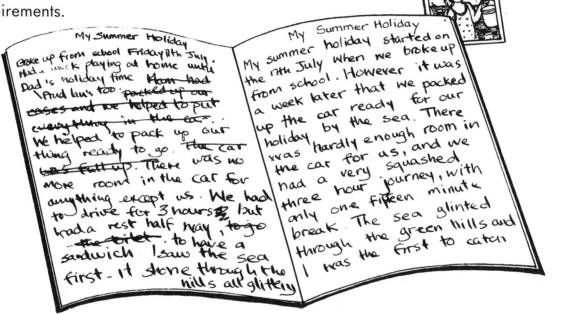

## What to do
Another way of helping children keep their writing decipherable when revising it is to get them to use the two pages of a double-page spread in an exercise book for different purposes. They can use the left hand page for notes, early drafts, experiments etc and then use the right hand page for more nearly completed writing.

## Follow-up
These books will inevitably still look somewhat messy, after a few pieces of writing. They will, however, be very good testimonies to the hard work done by the children in their writing. Don't hide them away on parents' evenings, but show them off to parents with an explanation of what they involve.

# Beginning revision

## Age range
Six to eleven.

## Group size
Individuals.

## What you need
No special requirements.

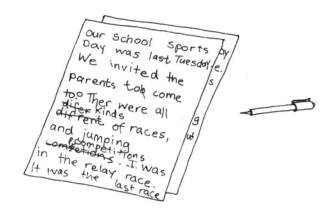

## What to do
The first step in encouraging children to revise their writing is to ensure that every time they complete an assignment, they read it through to themselves before presenting it to the teacher. This will often lead to them noticing the majority of their technical errors, such as misspellings, without the teacher having to correct them.

## Follow-up
Ask children to read through their writing pretending that they are the readers rather than the writers. This will often let them see for themselves points at which some revision is necessary.

# The writing conference

## Age range
Six to eleven.

## Group size
Individuals.

## What you need
No special requirements.

## What to do
When children are engaged in writing, circulate around the class, discussing with individuals what they are writing about, how their writing is going, how they feel about it and what they are going to write next. Do not focus too much on technical aspects, although there is a place for teaching technical skills during writing conferences.

Regular writing conferences do not entirely replace the marking of children's work. They are a valuable source of information for the teacher about the writing development of individual children, as well as being valuable for children as a real, concerned audience for their writing and a context for testing out ideas.

## Follow-up
When children are writing, you may find that your time is spent largely in writing conferences with them. This inevitably means you will not have time to deal with as many problems, such as spellings, as your did before. The children will therefore have to be trained to become more independent. Some ideas for doing this will be found in the section on technical skills (pages 86–93), but perhaps the most important thing is for the children to perceive writing conferences as so useful to them that they can appreciate the need not to interrupt them.

# Handling writing conferences

### Age range
Six to eleven.

### Group size
Individuals.

### What you need
No special requirements.

### What to do
- It is best to sit side by side with children during conferences, and as close to the same level as possible. This is to convey the idea that you are equal partners in this enterprise, and that the teacher is not the dominant one with all the answers.
- Do not take the children's pieces of writing from them. This will only signal that the responsibility for improving it is yours, not theirs. Instead, wait to be offered or shown the writing by the children.
- Let the children open the conversation about their writing. This will probably not happen to begin with, as the children will be unused to this order of events. At first you can begin with a neutral question to give children something to say. Ask: 'How is it going?' or 'Well, how are you getting on?' These should be open-ended enough to allow the conversation to begin and then develop in the way the children determine.
- During the conference, follow the children. Rather than impose your own perceptions upon the writing and the conversation, allow what the children say to determine the way things develop. Do not be afraid of giving your opinions about the writing, but do not expect the children to share them, or to immediately act upon them. Until children themselves can see the relevance of certain points, any changes you get them to make will be purely cosmetic and will not indicate real learning.

● Try to really *listen* to children during their writing conferences. To be of any help to them with their writing, you need to understand what their preoccupations are and how they see things. There is a direct relationship between the amount you as teacher learn about them, and the amount they themselves learn.

● Beware of the temptation during writing conferences not to give children sufficient time to think about what they are going to say about their writing. This is especially relevant when asking them direct questions. Most teachers find it extremely difficult to allow children periods of silence of longer than 30 seconds in which to think and formulate what they will say. Be prepared to sometimes allow over a minute for this. Once children know that you will allow them time to think, they, in turn, will give more time to thinking, and will be less inclined to give you hastily formulated and half-considered answers. This is crucial to writing development, which depends on children's willingness to reflect.

- When discussing children's writing with them, the main thing to look for is potential. Focus on points at which you think children could elaborate or expand upon their ideas. Look for occasions when children have expressed ideas well, praise them, and ask them if they could use this means of expression elsewhere. Do not concentrate on negative aspects of children's writing. This is easy to do almost without being aware of it, but will tend to reinforce children's negative feelings about their writing abilities. Try to look for positive points in every piece of writing, no matter how hard this might be. This does not, of course, mean ignoring the faults in children's writing, but attention to these should come near the end of the process, and children will often spot and remedy them themselves if given time.
- During the conference try to ask children questions that might teach rather than test them. Questions that do this will probably be either content or process questions.
- Content questions will focus on *what* is being said in the writing. Children need to develop ideas about what they are writing about before they can really work out how to write them. So questions which encourage them to think further about what they know, about their feelings towards it and about what might interest other people most about it, will help them think through more carefully what they want to say. These kinds of questions are also likely to be genuine questions, in that the children will know the answers better than the teacher. This, again, will encourage children to feel that they have ownership of their writing.

42

- Process questions will focus on *how* ideas are expressed on paper. Ask questions such as, 'Why did you mention this just here?', 'Do you think it would be better to say this before that?', 'What will you write next about this?' These will encourage children to reflect directly upon the way they express things, and help develop their abilities to become aware of the effects of what they write upon their audience.
- Use the writing conference as a context in which to teach specific writing skills. Because the children are engaged in real writing tasks, skill instruction is much more likely to have an effect. Skills such as the recognition and correct use of sentences, the use of punctuation marks and for older children, the use of paragraphs, can all be worked on during writing conferences. This will not be the main purpose of the conference, so do not devote so much time to skill teaching that the children think this more important than the meaningful dialogue about their writing intentions; this is what conferences are really about. It is probably best to focus on one skill per conference, at the most. This means that in many conferences, there will be no skill teaching. Dealing with writing skills this way, rather than through sets of disconnected exercises, will mean it will take longer to cover all the skills, but those skills that are covered will have a much greater chance of actually being absorbed.

## Follow-up

If you make a brief record of the kinds of skills which you needed to teach children during their writing conferences, then you will be able to base subsequent skill teaching on what children really need, rather than on the next exercise in the book.

# Collaborative long story writing

## Age range
Nine to eleven.

## Group size
Whole class.

## What you need
No special requirements.

## What to do
Decide beforehand on a broad plot outline for a story. Present this to the class, and allow time for discussion to sharpen up the details of the plot and elaborate upon the characters and situations involved. Discuss the descriptions of the setting, and divide it up into sections or chapters. Assign chapters to groups of children, or maybe to individuals. The groups have to produce their own chapters, but they have to ensure that the whole story fits together. This means that there needs to be constant communication between groups, and comparisons of the way each chapter is developing. You could also hold several whole class sessions to discuss development. The need to ensure fit will neccesitate a great deal of revising and editing.

## Follow-up
After working as a whole class, an individual child, or a small group of children, might want to take on the task themselves.

44

# A marathon write

## Age range
Seven to eleven.

## Group size
Whole class.

## What you need
No special requirements.

## What to do
Challenge children to write as many sentences as possible in a ten to fifteen minute period. Tell them that nobody is to ask about spellings; they are simply to write what they think. They will not be obliged to show their writing to anyone afterwards unless they wish to; neither will anyone ask them to 'write up' their ideas into any other form, although they may use the ideas later as a source for other writing. The aim of this activity is simply to get children to accept that everybody has something to write about, and not every piece of writing has to be polished and complete. Some ideas may only be useful as a starting point for others.

## Follow-up
A next step to this idea is to ask children to write for a set time about a particular subject. They may go on to share their ideas with other children in the class as part of a brainstorming session before collaborative writing.

# Three page stories

## Age range
Six to nine.

## Group size
Whole class.

## What you need
No special requirements.

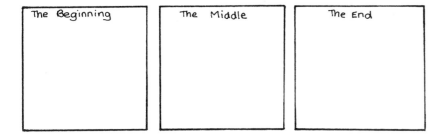

## What to do
Give the children three separate pieces of paper on which to write. Provide a suitable stimulus for a starting point, and get them to title the first sheet, 'Beginning', the second, 'Middle', and the third, 'End'. Tell them they are to write their stories in these three sections. Encourage discussion before they begin to write, and especially encourage them to plan beforehand which parts of their story should go on to which page. Each page could be accompanied by a picture, which could either be done before writing, as a rehearsal of their ideas or after writing, as an illustration of that part of the story.

# Using flow diagrams

## Age range
Seven to eleven.

## Group size
Individuals.

## What you need
No special requirements.

## What to do
Demonstrate to children how a flow diagram can be used to plan a story, or indeed any piece of writing. Begin with simple, linear diagrams such as:

Later children could be introduced to more complex diagrams, and could be shown how to write stories based upon them. For example:

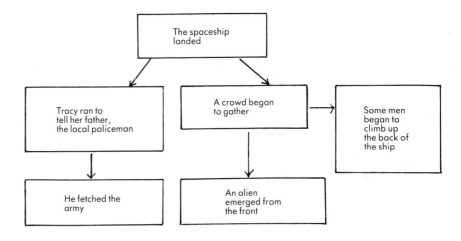

# Writing for a purpose

# Dialogue journals

**Age range**
Five to eleven.

**Group size**
Individuals.

**What you need**
A small exercise book
for each child.

**What to do**
Establish regular written communication with children through a book which they keep. The book can be used specially for this purpose, or it might also function as their 'news' book.

Ask the children to write something to you – a piece of news or something about themselves. Instead of marking it, you must respond to what it says with your own comments. This response might include a question or two to stimulate further writing from the children, although you will probably find that, once they are sure they have a real audience, the children will write quite readily. The books go back to the children, who continue the dialogue. This writing is private to the teacher and the individual child, although there is nothing to stop it being used in other ways, should children wish.

If this becomes a regular activity, it can obviously become very time-consuming for the teacher. One way of minimising this is to divide the class into three groups, and allot one week in turn to each group. This way every child will have a written dialogue with their teacher every three weeks.

# Writing instructions

## Age range
Six to eleven.

## Group size
Small groups of three to four children.

## What you need
No special requirements.

## What to do
Groups of children can work together to produce sets of written instructions for doing a range of activities. They might, for example, produce a set of rules for playing noughts and crosses, or draughts, or they might write step-by-step guides to operating such equipment as an instamatic camera, or a cassette recorder. They might also write instructions for such things as wiring a plug, or boiling an egg. Make sure they realise how important it is to get their instructions clear and precise. They can be told they are writing them for someone who has no idea about how to do these things. You will find that their instructions will be clearer if they are allowed to practise the activities they are writing about, and to try out their instructions on other children before producing final drafts.

## Follow-up
If the instructions the children write are later actually used by other children this will give their writing a real purpose. The instructions can be used as resource material for reading comprehension activities by other children. They can be used for other children simply to follow them.

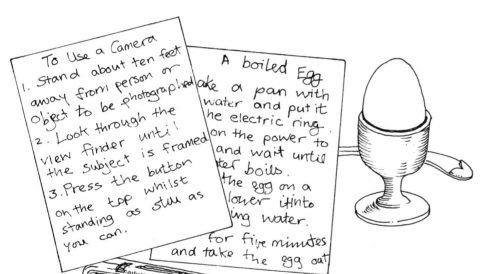

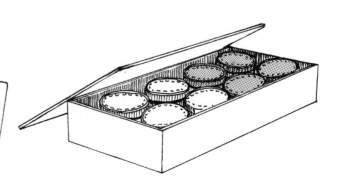

48

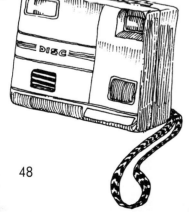

# The directions game

## Age range
Six to eleven.

## Group size
Whole class or small groups.

## What you need
No special requirements.

## What to do
Get a child to describe as precisely as possible how to move from one point in the classroom to several others to either carry out activities or to pick up certain objects. This description is written on a piece of card, which is then used by another child to try to follow the same actions exactly. Any points where the directions are inaccurate or ambiguous can be discussed, and the written directions altered.

## Follow-up
If the directions are written down precisely enough it ought to be possible for a blindfold child to follow them as they are read aloud. Children can try this and discuss the kind of precision they need to include in their writing.

# The construction game

## Age range
Six to eleven.

## Group size
Pairs of children.

## What you need
Two sets of construction materials, eg two sets of Lego, Meccano etc or two toy farms, or dolls' houses.

## What to do
The set of materials is arranged in a certain way by one child. Without the other seeing, the same child has then to write a description of the arrangement. The materials are then hidden from view. The description is given to the other child who has to try to arrange the second set of materials into exactly the pattern described. When the second child is satisfied the description has been followed, the first set of materials is uncovered, and both sets compared. If there are any discrepancies, both children rewrite the description to make it more accurate.

## Follow-up
This activity can obviously be followed through into children's other descriptive writing, whether this is done as part of story writing, or as an activity in its own right. Ask them to try to describe scenes or characters so that someone else could visualise exactly what they looked like.

# Giving directions

### Age range
Seven to eleven.

### Group size
Pairs of children.

### What you need
Large scale plans of the streets around the school. Make sure that the children understand the idea of street plans. This will involve some initial preparation work.

### What to do
One child writes a description of how to get from his or her house to the school. The other child has to follow this description on the plan. Afterwards both children evaluate the preciseness and accuracy of the written description. These may then need to be modified.

### Follow-up
There are many possibilities for other activities using this basic format. For example, the children might think about how to get from the school to the shops, or from the post office to the railway station, and so on.

The activity can also, of course, be done orally. Children can then compare the effectiveness of written and spoken directions. They might begin to realise that the problem with spoken directions is that, although they can be given in a way that fits exactly the needs of the listener, they do have to be remembered correctly. When the instructions are complicated this can be very difficult. Written directions avoid this memory problem, but have their own problems. The writer has to try to get everything perfectly clear before handing over the directions.

# Writing letters

## Age range
Six to eleven.

## Group size
Individuals or the whole class.

## What you need
No special requirements.

## What to do
Children need to be taught the conventions of letter writing, but they will learn these more effectively if the letters they write are actually for sending. There are many possibilities.

Children can write letters to parents to:

- invite them to open evenings;
- give details of class trips;
- tell them about things they are doing in school;
- tell about books they have read.

They can also write letters to:

- firms and other organisations requesting information about topics they are working on;
- other schools as part of a pen-friend scheme;
- authors and poets about what they have read (these can be sent c/o the publisher);
- places they have visited to say 'thank you' and to give some details of the work they have done in follow-up;
- visitors to the school.

## Follow-up
Hopefully the children will receive replies to many of the letters they send. These replies, as well as being interesting in their own right and a source of valuable reading practice, can also be used for discussion of writing. Look at how these letters are set out. How are they begun and ended? Are they written in any different way to the letters you wrote?

# Planning a class trip

### Age range
Eight to eleven.

### Group size
Whole class.

### What you need
A telephone directory, and a brochure about the selected destination.

### What to do
Much of the writing needed to organise the class trip can be done by the children themselves. You will probably need to do some initial surveying of dates, times and prices before letting the children loose. If the recipients are warned to expect them, the children can:

- work out dates which are most convenient for the trip;
- write to the location of the trip to book a date, and request any available prior information;
- find the address and telephone number of a local coach firm;
- phone the coach firm to enquire about prices and dates;
- write to confirm the date for the coach;
- write to the location of the trip to confirm the date;
- work out the total cost of the trip for the class;
- work out how much each of them will have to pay;
- write to parents requesting permission to go on the trip, informing them of the cost and the date by which money has to be paid;
- after the trip, plan how they will present their writing about their day (a useful idea is to get them to design their own version of the brochure);
- draft, edit and finally produce a written response to the trip;
- send a copy of their work, together with a letter of thanks, to the host's location and to anyone else you think should have one.

### Follow-up
Naturally the children will make mistakes in doing all of this. The teacher will need to make sure that these mistakes do not affect the smooth running of the trip itself, but can use the mistakes as valuable starting points for teaching. Children are likely to be much keener to improve their abilities if they can see that it is really important to get things right.

# Writing for younger children

### Age range
Seven to eleven.

### Group size
Whole class or any sized group.

### What you need
Access to a class of children at least two years younger than your own.

### What to do
Discuss with your children the kinds of things they liked to read when they were younger. When they have some ideas they can go along to the younger class, a few at a time, to talk individually to a younger child. During this time they have to find out about what the younger child likes to do, what he or she is interested in, and the kinds of stories he/she most likes to read. They will need to note this information down. When they come back to class, discuss with them what they have found and the kind of story they might be able to write for their adopted youngster. They can then begin writing, either alone or in groups of two or three. They may change their story as much as they like, and perhaps have several alternative versions. When they are ready, they go back to their youngster to read their story to him/her. How the younger child receives it, and how he/she reacts to it will give them further information. When they return to class, they can then make any necessary alterations to the stories, and produce them in a version which the younger child can take away and read alone. This final version will need to be illustrated, which the children can either do themselves, or with cut-out pictures.

### Follow-up
This activity will become more beneficial the more the children do it, since they will get to know more and more about the reading likes and dislikes of their adopted child. The books they produce can be kept by the younger child, or be added to the library of the younger class. The older children thus get the thrill of seeing a book by themselves on the shelves, and the younger children get an extra book to read.

# A class newspaper 1

### Age range
Six to eleven.

### Group size
Whole class or groups of around six children.

### What you need
Access to a typewriter, preferably a jumbo. A set of Letraset letters, or a large letter stencil.

### What to do
Get the children to produce a class newspaper with reports of newsworthy events in school and in the locality, such as school functions, sports matches, achievements etc. Also advertisements for forthcoming events. The newspaper should also carry reports on neighbourhood activities such as fêtes, cinema films, theatrical productions, sporting events, fun runs etc. Assign children to produce particular contributions. The final copy can be typed on the jumbo typewriter, and Letraset letters or stencils used for the headlines. If you can make copies of the newspaper, you could sell it to children for a few pence.

### Follow-up
While producing a newspaper, children will be studying real newspapers. Bring several into class, and discuss the purpose of the various sections. Arrange a visit to a local newspaper office or invite a reporter on a local newspaper into class to talk about his or her work.

# A class newspaper 2

## Age range
Six to eleven.

## Group size
Whole class or groups of around six children.

## What you need
Access to a typewriter, preferably a jumbo. A set of Letraset letters, or a large letter stencil.

## What to do
When the children have some notion of what producing a newspaper involves, they are ready to take on more prescribed roles in the production of their own. The class could be divided up into three, or perhaps four teams. One team can be designated as reporters with the responsibility for finding events on which to report, and writing those reports. Another team can be the editorial section, with responsibility for advising the reporters on the length, content and accuracy of their reports. They would also act as proof-readers. A further team can be responsible for the design of the newspaper, deciding on the layout and the use of pictures. If possible, a fourth team could be responsible for advertisements. This needs to be done with care, and with the first contacts made by the teacher, but sometimes it is possible to get local shops or businesses to place advertisements in school and class newspapers. Sometimes these people will pay a small amount for the privilege, and this will help cover the costs of duplicating the newspaper. If this happens, make sure that these contributors get a free copy of the newspaper with their advertisement in.

## Follow-up
If a computer and a printer are available for use, these can be used in the production of a newspaper. There are several software packages available which will assist with this.

# A class magazine

### Age range
Six to eleven.

### Group size
Whole class or groups.

### What you need
A typewriter, preferably jumbo. Some means of duplicating type-written sheets, and, if possible, pictures.

### What to do
A class or school magazine can be produced along similar lines to the class newspaper. The magazine would, however, contain more 'creative' forms of writing. It would include children's earlier work as well as writing done specially for the magazine. Children should know if their work is going to be included, and be given the opportunity to alter/polish it if they wish. A selection team could be appointed from the class to choose suitable work for the magazine; the teacher will need to have some influence here to get work included which is perhaps not outstanding in an absolute sense, but is good for the child who produced it. An editorial/proof-reading team and a design team will also be needed, as for the newspaper. It is possible to produce black and white duplicated copies of drawings reasonably easily on a photocopier, or on a spirit duplicator if the children draw directly onto the master sheet.

### Follow-up
If the magazine is duplicated and distributed fairly widely, you should charge a few pence for it. This not only covers the cost of production, but also ensures that those who receive it do value it. Nothing can be more disheartening for children who are proud that their work has been chosen for the magazine than to see the streets outside school littered with discarded free copies.

# The notice-board

## Age range
Six to eleven.

## Group size
Flexible.

## What you need
A spare piece of pin-board, placed where it is likely to be seen by most children either in the school or in one class.

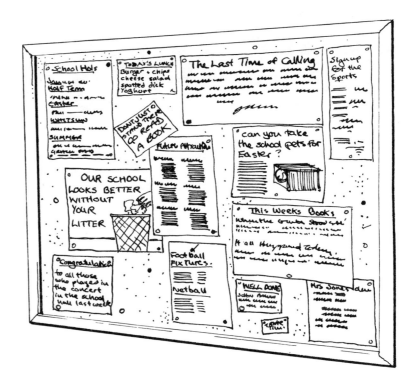

## What to do
Establish a class or a school notice-board to which children contribute. You could have a notice-board committee consisting of children and a teacher to decide which contributions could go on the notice-board and how they should be arranged. Items which children could write for the notice-board include:—

- notices advertising school events,
- school lunch menus,
- dates of school holidays,
- notices about how to look after the school pets,
- messages of congratulations, eg 'Well done to the school football team for scoring four goals in their last match', or, 'Congratulations to these people for their excellent play in assembly last week',
- posters such as, 'Our school looks better without your litter', or, 'Don't just stand and look, go and read a book',
- book jackets and information about the week's featured book.

# Types of writing

# Starting points for poetry

## Structured poetry

**Age range**
Six to eleven.

**Group size**
Whole class.

**What you need**
No special requirements.

**What to do**
Ask the children to find something small to write about. This can be a living or an inanimate object. Ask them to examine their object very carefully. They can use a hand-lens or microscope if they wish. Then ask them five questions about their object, and tell them their answers will be written on separate lines and will form five-line poems. The questions are:

- what colour is it?
- what does it look like?
- what does it remind you of?
- what is it used for?
- is it heavy or light?

**Follow-up**
The exercise can be repeated several times, using different objects and, eventually, different questions.

Pebble

Grey-blue
Huddled mouse,
You remind me of sugared almonds.
You have no use.
You are heavier than my budgie and lighter than my gerbil.

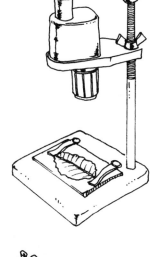

# Furniture poetry

**Age range**
Six to eleven.

**Group size**
Whole class.

**What you need**
No special requirements.

**What to do**
Ask the children to think about a person they know well.
The teacher may be the best person to begin with as the
results are likely to be quite amusing. Tell them that each
line of the poem they write will say:

- what piece of furniture this person is like,
- what time of day,
- what kind of fruit,
- what sort of weather,
- what kind of animal.

**Follow-up**
This can be played as a game if the poems are written
about people in the class without mentioning any names.
Listeners have to try to guess who is being referred to.

Ask them to write the poem.

**Grandma**
My grandma's like an armchair, warm and cosy near the
fire,
Like storytime before the night when everyone is tired.
She's like a winter apple, wrinkled but yet sweet,
A rich white blanket-snowy day, a cat on velvet feet.

# Alphabet poetry

## Age range
Six to eleven.

## Group size
Whole class.

## What you need
No special requirements.

> ### Autumn
> a   Autumn is a season
> b   blustery weather battering the trees
> c   chilly winds cool the air
> d   dull and rainwashed days
> e   evenings getting darker
> f   falling leaves flutter down

## What to do
This is an ideal way to begin group poetry. Write the letters of the alphabet down the side of the blackboard. Decide between you on a suitable topic to write about. Ask the children to choose some letters, and to write interesting lines beginning with these about the topic. When they have done five or six each, go through the alphabet together, taking suggestions for each letter. Discuss the relative merits of each suggestion, ask for any improvements which might be made, and choose interesting examples to go towards the communal poem.

# Acrostics

## Age range
Six to eleven.

## Group size
Whole class.

## What you need
No special requirements.

## What to do
Acrostic poetry provides a well-structured format within which most children can produce interesting poetry. Begin by choosing a keyword. The children can each choose their own, or one can be used for the whole class. The keyword is written downwards on the left side of the page. Children then have to write a poem using the keyword as a theme, in which each line begins with a letter of the keyword.

> ### Snow
> S ilver, satin, so silent,
> n o noise except crunch, crunch.
> O h, how the sound lives.
> w hy does the noise make that sound ?

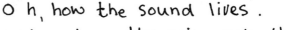

> ### Misty
> Magically it rises
> I nto the unknown darkness
> S himmering and creeping. all done,
> T ogether you and I
> Y earn for somewhere safer.

# Acrostic introductions

## Age range
Six to eleven.

## Group size
Whole class.

## What you need
No special requirements.

## What to do
For the first lesson with a new class, many teachers get children to write about themselves. A variation on this is to get them to write in acrostic form. They can use their own name as the keyword and then proceed as in the previous idea.

P eter
E ats everything he can find
T alks all the time in class
E ven fights a bit outside, but
R eally is a nice boy when he likes.

T racey
r arely does what she's told
a lways talks too loudly
c an be very funny
e ven when she's sad
y es, she's a friendly girl.

# Calligrams

## Age range
Five to eleven.

## Group size
Any.

## What you need
No special requirements.

## What to do
A calligram is a word written on the page in such a way that its shape reflects its meaning. Here are some examples:

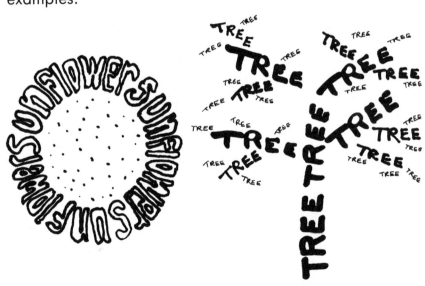

Ask the children to try to make calligrams from such words as:
spooky  shivery  zoom  zig-zag  pop
twinkling  lollipop  crash  rainbow

# Shape poems 1

**Age range**
Six to eleven.

**Group size**
Any.

**What you need**
No special requirements.

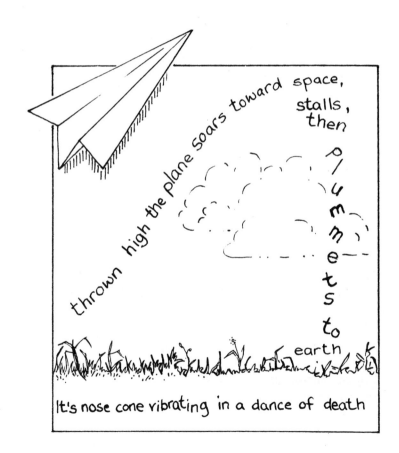

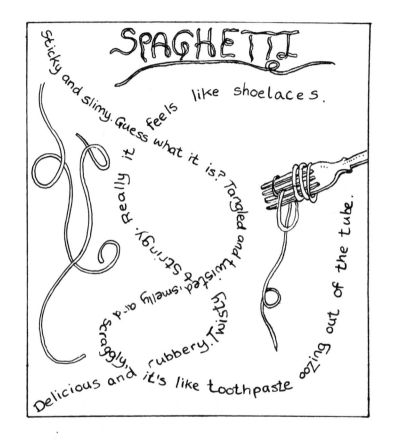

## What to do
In shape poems the way in which the poem is written on the page reflects its theme. Many people will be familiar with the fine examples of this written by the French poet, Guillaume Apollinaire. Here are some examples of ideas produced by children.

# Shape poems 2

**Age range**
Six to eleven.

**Group size**
Any.

**What you need**
No special requirements.

**What to do**
Most poems can be written as shape poems. Get the children to begin by drawing or tracing a shape connected with their poem. They then write their poem around the outline of the shape. Obvious possibilities are: snake; worm; pyramid; star; staircase; butterfly; the sun; dragon; wheel; cat.

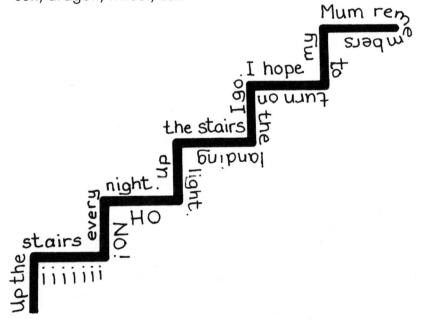

# List poems

**Age range**
Six to eleven.

**Group size**
Any.

**What you need**
No special requirements.

**What to do**
List poems are relatively easy to produce and lend themselves well to group poetry. Begin with a theme such as 'Happiness', 'Friendship', 'Spring' etc. Children have to write lines on this theme, each line beginning with the word. For example:

**Happiness**
Happiness is awakening to find it's snowed,
Happiness is a bunch of grapes when you are ill.
Happiness is going with Grandad to see the match,
Happiness is finally reaching the top of the hill.

**Follow-up**
You can vary the format of each line to make it less repetitive, perhaps by every other line beginning with 'It . . .'. For example:

**Autumn**
Autumn is a season of surprises,
It's full of colours and of smells.
Autumn has its leaves of fire,
Its harvest and its fruit as well.

# Biting an apple

**Age range**
Six to eleven.

**Group size**
Any.

**What you need**
An apple per child.

**What to do**
Children need an apple each which they can then go on to eat. Instruct them to:

- give one word to describe what the apple looks like.
- close their eyes and give one word about how the apple feels to touch.
- take a bite. Give one word to describe the sound as their teeth bit the apple.
- give one word to describe the taste.
- swallow. Write a sentence describing how it makes their mouths feel.

Write their five-lined poems on apple shapes.

Shiny , silky, crunchy, sharply tingling on my tongue.

Rough, hairy , crisp. Sweet . Mouth watering Fresh and.

**Follow-up**
Do the same with other fruit and vegetables such as a lemon, a potato, a carrot etc.

# Sensing emotions

### Age range
Six to eleven.

### Group size
Any.

### What you need
No special requirements.

### What to do
Tell children to think of an emotion such as fear, happiness, anger etc, and to write a poem about this emotion according to the following formula:

- what colour is this emotion?
- what does it taste like?
- what does it smell like?
- what does it look like?
- what does it sound like?
- what does it feel like?

**Fear**
My fear is red as the evening sky,
It tastes of black, burned toast.
It smells of bonfires, looks like bonfires,
Sounds like an animal about to die.
It's jagged, harsh and makes me cry.

# Alliterative sentences

### Age range
Six to eleven.

### Group size
Any.

### What you need
No special requirements.

### What to do
Get the children to write sentences in which particular sounds feature largely. For example:

seven sorrowful skiers sitting in soft snow.

nine nervous nitwits nibbling nice new nuts.

### Follow-up
Children could try doing this with sentences beginning with specific letters in sequence. Counting down from ten to one, or up from one to ten is popular. Try it with the colours of the rainbow, or the letters of the alphabet.

# Haiku

## Age range
Seven to eleven.

## Group size
Any.

## What you need
No special requirements.

## What to do
Haiku is a Japanese form of poetry. Strictly each Haiku should have 17 syllables, five in the first line, seven in the second, and five in the third. However, this does not matter too much as long as children keep the lines short and try to pack as much meaning into them as possible. They could also be asked to try to get a surprising image in the last line. Here are some attempts at Haiku, none of which are in the strict form.

**Winter**
The winter
The winter will blow
The snow will clean all the air.

**The Book**
See the book
Waiting to be read
Come on in it will swallow you.

**Snow**
The sun comes
It melts the white snow
The grass is cleaned by the snow.

## Follow-up
Children can try other strict forms of poetry. Japanese Tanka, or English Cinquains can be used. These each have their peculiar restrictions and children will enjoy the challenge of trying to keep within them.

# Descriptive writing

## Flow chart writing

**Age range**
Six to eleven.

**Group size**
Whole class.

**What you need**
No special requirements.

**What to do**
Begin with an object or an event which children are to describe. Get them to think of words or phrases to describe it. The work is then displayed with a picture representing what is being described in the centre, and the words and phrases the children have thought of coming out of it in flow chart fashion.

Flickering through the trees.

Silvery white.

Mysterious, dark patterns.

Eerie, ghostly light on the lawn.

The Moon

White cold with hard edges.

Shining silver on the sea.

# Getting into focus

## Age range
Eight to eleven.

## Group size
Whole class.

## What you need
A slide of a scene; slide projector; examples of children's descriptive writing (anonymous) with not very precise descriptions.

## What to do
Show the slide and get the children to describe orally what they can see in as much detail as possible.

Afterwards show the slide slightly out of focus so that few details can be seen. Read out a piece of writing in which the descriptions are not very precise. Compare this to the out-of-focus slide, in that both enable few details to be clearly perceived by reader or viewer. Sharpen the slide's focus, and ask the children if they can sharpen the focus of their descriptions.

# Descriptions from pictures

### Age range
Seven to eleven.

### Group size
Whole class.

### What you need
A collection of interesting and detailed pictures.

### What to do
Get children to write descriptions of what they see in their pictures. Then get them to share their descriptions with a partner with the aim of making them more precise and more detailed.

The next step is to get other children to try to draw pictures from these descriptions. It does not matter if these pictures are artistic or not. The picture-drawers and the description-writers come together to discuss the success of the activity. They are not evaluating drawing skill but whether the writing gave sufficient details for the people drawing to get as close as possible to the original pictures.

### Follow-up
Attempting to draw pictures as a result of reading descriptions in books is a useful reading exercise and also a good way of illustrating the importance of detailed descriptions.

70

# Who am I?

**Age range**
Six to eleven.

**Group size**
Whole class.

**What you need**
No special requirements.

**What to do**
Get children to describe themselves as accurately as they can in three simple sentences. Read out several of these descriptions and see if the rest of the class can guess who the subjects are each time.

**Follow-up**
If the children do cut-out silhouettes of their heads, their three-sentence descriptions can be mounted alongside these, in a 'Who am I?' display.

Who am I ?

I am 9 years old
I am a boy with short
spiky hair.

I wear one pony tail
I have blue eyes
and freckles

I have my hair in
bunches every day
I wear earrings.

# Observational writing

**Age range**
Six to eleven.

**Group size**
Whole class.

**What you need**
A collection of interesting objects.

**What to do**
Observational drawing can be accompanied and extended by getting children to try to describe their objects in words. Ask them to concentrate on aspects such as texture, colour etc. Completed descriptions can be displayed alongside their drawings.

**Sara's Shell**

**The Shell**
The shell is called a Cowrie shell. It has got spots on it and is pink inside. The lips are ridged. It is very smooth all over. An animal used to live in it.

**Stuart's Star Fish**

**The Star Fish**
My star fish has gone hard now but once it was soft and fleshy. It has got five points. They are not all the same size.

**Sam's Sea Weed**

**The Sea Weed**
Black, stringy, smelly sea weed. It has small round blobs that burst if you squeeze them and ooze slimy liquid.

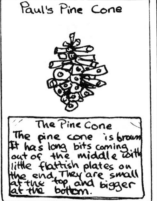
**Paul's Pine Cone**

**The Pine Cone**
The pine cone is brown. It has long bits coming out of the middle with little flattish plates on the end. They are small at the top and bigger at the bottom.

**Laura's Leaf**

**The Leaf**
The leaf has five points and two tiny points near the st... As well as green the leaf has got some brown and red in it and yellow tips. It has veins running along...

**Hari's Holly**

**The Holly**
...een prickly holly ...ed berries. We ...Christmas to ...our homes. ...shiny almost ...waxy leaf.

# Story writing

## Using the story wheel

**Age range**
Seven to eleven.

**Group size**
Individuals or groups of three to four.

**What you need**
Cut out and assemble the story wheel from page 120 or design a similar one of your own.

**What to do**
The story wheel in this book focuses on communication. Others could be designed using the same idea.

Get the children to 'dial up' a situation and use it as a basis for a story. For example, they might dial up the grandmother sending the message 'It's going to be twins', through a megaphone to the film-goer. What might the story behind this be?

**Follow-up**
This particular story wheel could be a starting point for discussion about the effects of the media we choose for the messages we wish to pass on. Are some media more, or less appropriate for certain messages?

## Using the story chart

**Age range**
Six to eleven.

**Group size**
Individuals or groups of three to four.

**What you need**
A copy of the story chart to be found on page 121.

**What to do**
Children can follow through a particular path on the chart which will give them the ingredients for a story. They can write this individually or in collaboration with other children.

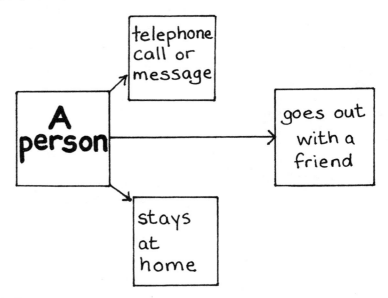

**Follow-up**
Some children may go on to design their own story charts which could then be used with other children.

# Strip cartoons

### Age range
Six to eleven.

### Group size
Whole class.

### What you need
Copies of several well-known comics.

### What to do
Discuss with the children how stories are told in comics. Get them to tell a story that they have read in a comic. They can go on to tell their own stories through the comic strip cartoon format.

One night near Christmas, Jim and Ella were just going to bed, they looked out of the . . . very b . . .

One Night near Christmas Jim and Ella saw a bright star.

Next day they found a bright star in their garden.

They took it to show to their Mum in the house.

They said it had fallen out of the sky.

Mum s . . . off the . . .

### Follow-up
Some children may go on to write the comic stories they have produced in a more usual written form. These can be displayed, perhaps in the format used by the famous Rupert Bear cartoons in the *Daily Express*, in which the pictures are accompanied by text at two levels, a very simple and a more complex one.

# Find a story

### Age range
Six to eleven.

### Group size
Individuals or groups of three to four.

### What you need
Three sets of cards. One set has names and descriptions of several interesting characters, eg Billy Buffalo, the cowboy with the wooden leg, or Katy Kangaroo, the bionic marsupial. A second has interesting times, eg the kick-off time in the Cup Final, or the last minute of school before the summer holidays. A third has interesting places, eg a tropical island in the South Seas, or a space station off Jupiter. These categories can be varied at will.

### What to do
Place each set of cards in a separate pack. Children have to choose one card from each pack, and then use them as a starting point for a story.

### Follow-up
Children can go on to add their own cards to the sets.

# Informative writing

## Writing advertisements

### Age range
Seven to eleven.

### Group size
Whole class.

### What you need
Several examples of advertisements from newspapers and magazines.

### What to do
Begin by looking at a range of advertisements with the children. Discuss what makes them attractive and why they may persuade people to buy what they are advertising. The children can then choose a product and, either individually or in small groups, write an advertisement for that product, trying to persuade people to buy it.

### Follow-up
The class can discuss the advertisements that emerge, and suggest improvements, or go on to plan an advertising campaign to include such things as siting, size etc. This campaign can be related to a product of educational value. For example, the class might mount an advertising campaign to persuade people to buy the school magazine.

# Designing posters

### Age range
Six to eleven.

### Group size
Whole class.

### What you need
No special requirements.

### What to do
Get the children to design posters to communicate some information important to them. This could range from the date and time of the next school football match, to a notice about their forthcoming class assembly, or an advertisement for a book they found particularly interesting. In any case, get them to ask the following questions:

- will the reader understand the poster?
- does it include all the essential information?
- is it designed appropriately, ie are the illustrations right? What about the lettering?

### Follow-up
Children should canvass the opinions of other children on their work, to answer these questions.

# Personal passports

## Age range
Six to eleven.

## Group size
Whole class.

## What you need
One or more passports as examples.

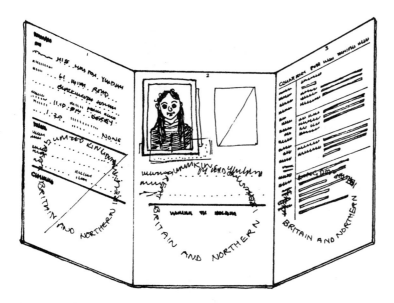

## What to do
Children can write their own personal passports. Begin by showing them a real passport, and discuss the kind of personal information it contains. Let the children copy the format into a small booklet of their own, and then fill in the various pieces of information. The photograph can either be a real one brought from home or they can draw a self-portrait.

## Follow-up
If you can obtain some passport application forms from local post offices, children can practise filling these in. They can then pass on the form to another child who can act as passport issuer, checking the information on the form against that on the passport, and then giving the latter an official stamp before issuing it.

# Designing menus

## Age range
Six to eleven.

## Group size
Whole class.

## What you need
Some examples of restaurant menus would help.

## What to do
Get the children to design attractive menus for an imaginary restaurant. They need to canvass opinion as to which kinds of food they should include, discuss ways of describing each dish as appetisingly as possible (eg 'fresh, mouth-watering fillets of cod, grilled to perfection in golden, crispy breadcrumbs, served with a tangy wedge of lemon'), and decide on appropriate names for the dishes (scampi écolière, or super-duper-king-size-extra-burger, for example). Finally they need to write the menu out in an attractive way, perhaps using Gothic script, or copperplate writing.

## Follow-up
The front of the menu could contain an advertisement for the restaurant itself. Children will need to decide on its selling points, and describe it appropriately. For example, they might emphasise its intimate atmosphere and first class cuisine, or its rapid service and its Superman decor.

# Tele-messages

### Age range
Seven to eleven.

### Group size
Whole class.

### What you need
No special requirements.

### What to do
Get the children to write messages passing on particular information using as few words as they can. You can have competitions to see who can get the message down to the fewest words without losing the meaning. Discuss the techniques the children use. What kinds of words are the more essential, and which add little to the meaning?

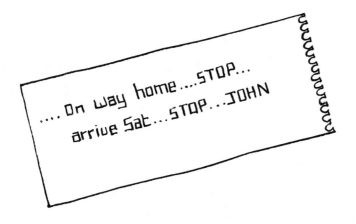

### Follow-up
Children can prepare these messages by using words cut out from newspapers. They might also discuss some of the confusions which might result from ambiguous messages of this kind.

Also look at telegrams and discuss the ways people use them to ensure that a message is conveyed when each word is precious.

# Inventing slogans

### Age range
Seven to eleven.

### Group size
Whole class.

### What you need
No special requirements.

### What to do
Show children several examples of the kind of competition in which you are asked to invent a phrase of less than ten, or less than 20 words to describe why some brand of chocolate/coffee/cereal/baked beans etc is more delicious than any other. Children could try this and maybe actually enter the competitions! Or they could perhaps try to make up this kind of slogan for things related to school. For example:

- why our class is the best in the school at writing.
- why our teacher is the nicest.
- why our classroom is the most exciting place to be.

If this is made into a competition, a small prize could be given for the entry the class decides is the most original.

Janine McLeod
Our teacher is the nicest because....
she doesn't shout at us so much as the others.

10 words

Chang Ling
teacher is the est because...
takes us on ol trips and ings.

ds

Roberta Johns
teacher is the est because of her nice clothes d her perfume.

9 words

7 words

# Miscellaneous writing ideas

## Ten writing games

### Age range
Six to eleven.

### Group size
Pairs of children or groups of various sizes.

### What you need
No special requirements.

### What to do
**Sentence expansion**
Write a short sentence. Now make the sentence longer by changing one of the words in it for two new words. For example, 'Mary sat on her chair', then 'Mary sat on her black cat'. Keep going and see how long you can make the sentence. Play with a friend if you like.

**Body rhymes**
'On my chest I have a nest',
'On my knee I have a flea'.
Make up funny sentences that rhyme describing what you have in or on different parts of your body. Ask a friend to help you.

**Inventing words**

Make up your own words. Ask a friend to help you. Make up angry words like 'sockrot', or pretty words like 'tingleswing', or silly words like 'flattyband'. Make up some sad words, gentle words, fierce words and so on.

## A long story

Get or make a very long strip of paper, long enough to go all round the classroom. Start writing. Can you reach the end of the strip? Ask a friend to help you.

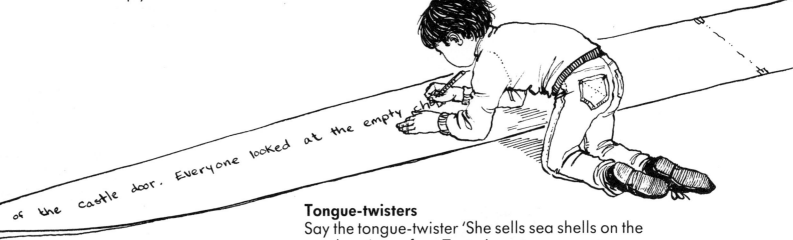

of the castle door. Everyone looked at the empty

the princess said to the plum and so saying she picked up her long

## Tongue-twisters

Say the tongue-twister 'She sells sea shells on the seashore' very fast. Try to invent your own tongue-twisting sentences and challenge your friend to say them fast.

## Comparisons game

With a friend, try to finish these sentences with a word or phrase. The first two are already done but you could change them if you like.

As miserable as . . . a centipede with chilblains.

As hairy as . . . a gorilla's armpit.

As dark as . . .

As sad as . . .

As daft as . . .

Now carry on and make up the beginnings of the sentences as well.

as hairy as

## Guess the meaning

Ask your friend to write a sentence for you with just one nonsense word in it. Like this, 'She closed her eyes and plixed him.' Now, you have to find as many words as possible that will replace the nonsense word and make the sentence make sense.

## Mobius sentence

Cut out a strip of paper about 1 cm wide and 50 cm long. Join it with just one twist and you have made a Mobius strip. It has only one side! Put your pencil on it and draw a line. You can go round without taking your pencil off. Some sentences are like this. Like this one . . . 'When you get out of a taxi the driver must smile and wait for a tip because he knows that when you get out of a . . .'. Try to make one of these up and write it onto a Mobius strip.

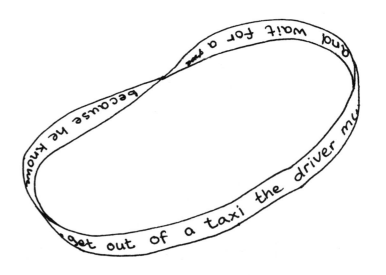

## Random word sentences
Sit with some friends. Each of you must write down any word you think of. Now, using all the different words you have written, plus some more if you need them, try to make up a sentence.

## Nonsense stories
Sit with about four friends. Each of you write a sentence on the top of your page. Pass your paper one person around the circle. The next person has to read your sentence and write a new sentence to follow it. He/she must then fold the paper so that the first sentence cannot be seen, and then pass the paper on. The next person repeats the process, writing a sentence to follow the one he can see, and then folding it over so that only the new sentence is visible. Do this a few times then read out the stories you have got.

# Technical skills of writing

# The word bank 1

## Age range
Five to nine.

## Group size
Individuals.

## What you need
Suitable pockets/boxes for storing word cards. These can be made from card or cloth and secured onto large charts of card, or directly onto the wall. Have one pocket for each letter of the alphabet, and prepare a set of initial cards on which are written words commonly used by children.

## What to do
As children are doing their writing and come to you requiring spellings, direct them first of all to the correct pocket of the word bank. After a time they should be able to do this for themselves. If the word they want is in the bank, they can either take it away to their seats and copy it into their writing, or, preferably, study it without taking it away and then try to write it from memory.

## Follow-up
Try-it-again sheets (see page 90) can be a useful way of reinforcing the spellings the children get from the word bank.

# The word bank 2

## Age range
Five to nine.

## Group size
Individuals.

## What you need
As for the previous activity.

## What to do
If the word the children want is not in the word bank, then write it for them on a blank piece of card. When they have finished with it, it can be added to the word bank for future use by other children.

If children are gradually trained to use other means of finding spellings, for example, dictionaries, they can begin to contribute to the word bank. Let them write words they find interesting, or which they think may be useful to others, to add to the word bank.

## Follow-up
The word bank will need regular maintenance. It will eventually be possible to remove words from it which the majority of the class are competent at spelling. This can be done in consultation with the children themselves. Perhaps a group of children – *not* the best spellers – can act as a word bank committee, and suggest words which they think can now be removed.

# The word bank 3

## Age range
Five to nine.

## Group size
Individuals.

## What you need
Each child needs a small exercise book. At the head of each page, write a letter of the alphabet.

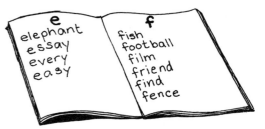

## What to do
When children come to you to ask for spellings ask them to bring their word books with them. Ask them, at the very least, to turn to the page of the book on which they think their word will go. Encourage them to look through their words to ensure that the one they want is not already there. You can either write the word for them on the page, or insist they try it themselves before showing it to you. This latter strategy is the more useful in the long term, because it encourages independence. Get them to hunt around for the words they want, using the class word bank or dictionaries. Very often you will need only to confirm their spelling. If they have got the word wrong, ensure the error is crossed out, and write in the correct spelling. You might get them to look carefully at the word, and then to practise it a few times, without looking, before they use it in their writing.

# Word charts

## Age range
Five to eight.

## Group size
Individuals.

## What you need
A large chart divided up into a grid. Squares of coloured paper.

## What to do
Above each column of the chart stick a different coloured square of paper. Alongside each row write the numbers, for example, up to ten. Inside each of the squares of the grid write a commonly used word. Pin the chart in a prominent place in the classroom. When children ask for the spellings of words which are on the chart, they can be given help at a variety of levels in locating them. They might be told, 'The word you want is in the green column', or, 'Look along row 4', or, more precisely, 'It's in the blue column and row 5'.

| | green | red | blue | yellow |
|---|---|---|---|---|
| 1 | was | said | there | it |
| 2 | and | the | had | again |
| 3 | once | never | Mummy | Daddy |
| 4 | brother | sister | baby | cat |
| 5 | car | road | house | dog |
| 6 | bus | lorry | under | above |

## Follow-up
You could prepare fresh charts of words which are likely to be in demand when working on a particular topic.

# Word boxes

**Age range**
Five to eight.

**Group size**
Table groups.

**What you need**
Sufficient plastic index boxes for one per table of children. A supply of index cards.

**What to do**
Put around 30 index cards into each group's box. Use one for each letter of the alphabet plus one each for the consonant digraphs TH, SH, CH and WH. Write the appropriate letter on each card. A set of alphabet cards, which often come free with the boxes, may also be useful, and will help teach children alphabet skills. You can begin by writing several likely words on the cards, or this can simply be done as and when children request them. When there are words on the cards, encourage children to help others on their table in locating the words they want. If these are not already on the cards, then it is likely that at least one child on the table will know the word, and can write it on to the right card. In this way children will be able to help each other with their spelling, rather than relying entirely on the teacher.

# Try-it-again sheets

**Age range**
Six to eleven.

**Group size**
Individuals.

**What you need**
Small exercise books with the pages folded, concertina-style, into four columns.

| word | try it here | try it again | and again |
|------|-------------|--------------|-----------|
| elephant porridge | elphant porig | elephent porrige | elephant porridge |

**What to do**
When children ask for a spelling which you consider they should learn, write it in the first column of this exercise book. Get the child to study it carefully and ask them to 'try to see it in your head'. When the child says he/she can do this, fold the page so that the word is hidden. The child then has to write the word from memory in the 'Try it here' column. If correct, the child can practise a couple more times in the extra columns, folding the page over each time. If wrong, the child looks again at the word and repeats the process. This is done until the word can be written correctly.

# Teaching speech marks

## Age range
Six to nine.

## Group size
Any size.

## What you need
Several comic strips with the characters' words written in balloons.

## What to do
Paint out the words inside the speech balloons, using liquid paper (See figure 1). Ask the children to guess what should be inside the balloons. (This is a very useful group reading exercise in its own right). They then write in the words they decide upon (See figure 2).

Figure 1

Figure 2

Then paint out part of the balloon around the speech, just leaving the two parts as in (See figure 3). Explain that these are left there just to show that the character is speaking. Make the marks look more like real speech marks (See figure 4).

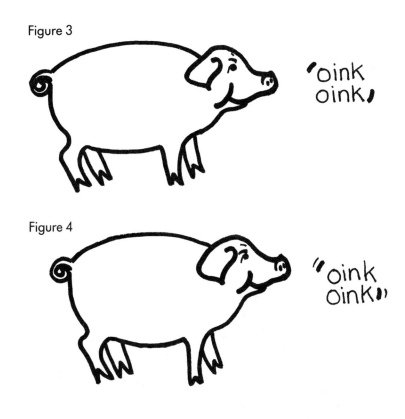

Figure 3

Figure 4

## Follow-up
Show the children speech marks in written conversation and explain that these are the remains of the speech balloons. See if they can do their own speech balloons.

# Illustrating metaphors

### Age range
Seven to eleven.

### Group size
Whole class.

### What you need
No special requirements.

### What to do
To get children to begin to appreciate the nature of metaphors and to use them more readily in their own writing, allow them to produce literal illustrations of popular ones. They could, for example, illustrate such things as 'He's got his head in the clouds', 'He laughed his head off', or 'Give me a hand'. Illustration could be followed by discussion about why these expressions are used, and the children could be asked to find similar use of metaphor in stories they read.

he's got his head in the clouds

Ha Ha Ha!

He laughed his head off

O.K. give me a hand

hand.

# Marking children's work

## Age range
Five to eleven.

## Group size
Individuals.

## What you need
No special requirements.

## What to do
Remember that the purpose of marking children's writing should be, firstly, to be a sensitive audience for what they have to say, and, secondly, to help them improve it. This has several implications:

- always comment on the message children have tried to communciate before other aspects.
- be positive about the good points in their writing, and about things they could improve.
- give them the opportunity to improve the writing if it is at all possible.
- do not give the impression that marking is a punitive exercise, but stress the positive aspects.
- if it is at all possible, mark children's writing alongside the children. There is far more chance then that the marking will have an effect.
- try to avoid using red pen for marking. This tends to be associated with punishment.
- avoid making children 'do their corrections'. There are other ways of dealing with spelling.
- if you feel you have to 'correct' children's writing, ensure that this is limited to what actually benefits the children.

# Using new technology

# Using the word processor

## Age range
Six to eleven.

## Group size
Individuals or small groups of three to four children.

## What you need
A computer with a word-processing facility. A printer. (Children can be introduced to word-processing without using a printer, but the real value comes from seeing their work printed out.)

## What to do
When children begin to use the word processor, it is not a good idea to over-burden them with too many of the facilities to begin with. Children will usually discover these themselves if they have access to the hand book. If they ask you specifically how to do certain things they should be told. Otherwise the important features to introduce are, in this order:

- using the Shift key to get capital letters;
- word wrap, so they do not bother about line ends;
- the delete key;
- the use of the cursor;
- the difference between Insert and Overwrite;
- how to insert blank lines;
- how to begin new paragraphs.

## Follow-up
Later on you can introduce further facilities, although some of these will not be needed very often. These are:

- Search and Replace facilities;
- centring text;
- left and right justification;
- other formatting functions eg altering line length;
- cut and paste;
- using tab stops;
- controlling print-out, eg altering print fonts;
- using standard document formats, eg standard letters in which the headings are already printed.

# Grouping at the word processor

### Age range
Six to eleven.

### Group size
Individuals or groups of three to four children.

### What you need
A computer with a word-processing facility. Preferably a printer.

### What to do
Get children to compose stories and other kinds of writing on the word processor in groups rather than individually on most occasions. This group-composition is also useful in other kinds of writing as it gives children a real chance to *think* about their writing, rather than simply dash it down. Sharing other people's ideas forces them to consider their own more carefully. Working in groups also, of course, means a more economic use of an expensive piece of equipment.

### Follow-up
When children are using the word processor for group-composition, you will need to be careful about the make-up of the groups for this. It is very easy for one child to dominate the others in his/her group, with the result that their ideas do not get a proper hearing. Sometimes groups will select themselves on the basis of friendship or interest in a particular topic but, if possible, it is probably best to choose groups according to personality rather than ability.

Put strong personalities together. They will argue forcibly, but it will ensure that neither gets their own way without having to really justify their ideas.

Altering group make-up can have several purposes. It may be possible for a child with good writing ideas, but little technical skill at writing, to benefit greatly from working with more technically able children. It may also be possible for several usually retiring children to work together with positive results.

Although children will use the word processor in small groups for the majority of the time, they will also need occasions when they write this way individually. More personal pieces of writing will require individual work, and occasionally the word processor will be of real use for this.

# Managing computer time

### Age range
Six to eleven.

### Group size
Individuals or groups of three to four children.

### What you need
A computer with word-processing facility. A printer.

### What to do
When children are using the word processor for writing it is best to let them use their limited time on the machine for entering text rather than for editing and revising. For this they can use a hard copy of their writing, which they can then revise away from the computer. This frees the computer for someone else to use. The first group can come back to it later to enter their revisions into their text and again take away a hard copy.

### Follow-up
If each member of the group takes a hard copy of a text they are working on, they can each think of their own possible revisions. They can even take the text home to do this. They can then come together to discuss one another's suggestions before agreeing on the revisions they will make.

# Word-processing hints 1

### Age range
Six to eleven.

### Group size
Individuals or groups of three to four children.

### What you need
A computer with word-processing facility. A printer.

### What to do
When children are writing using the word processor, the teacher will need to spend some time in discussing and aiding their revisions. This is probably best done away from the computer, using print-outs of the text the children are working on. It is a simple matter for children to take sufficient print-outs so that everyone, including the teacher, can have their own copy. When the discussion is over, the teacher will still have a copy of this draft of the children's work, plus any notes on it arising from the revision discussion (for suggestions on how to handle these writing conferences see page 40). This can be added to the teacher's records, and can give a useful indication of children's progress in a variety of writing skills.

# Word-processing hints 2

## Age range
Six to eleven.

## Group size
Individuals or groups of three to four children.

## What you need
A computer with word-processing facility. A printer.

## What to do
When children have finished their writing on the word processor, the facility to take multiple hard copies of it can be extremely valuable. The children can obviously have their own copies, which may go into their files or books. The teacher can have a copy for record purposes, and another copy, if desired, for display. A further copy may be taken to put into a school or class magazine, and finally a copy can go home for parents to keep.

# Word-processing hints 3

### Age range
Six to eleven.

### Group size
Individuals or groups of three to four children.

### What you need
A computer with word-processing facility, preferably a printer.

### What to do
Even when children claim to have finished a particular piece of writing, and final copies have been taken, it is best not to erase it from computer disk or tape for some time afterwards. Children often want to come back to writing they have previously done and revise it again. The word processor makes this particularly easy to do, and children should be encouraged in it.

### Follow-up
Children sometimes get so taken with the ease of revising writing on a word processor that they find it very difficult to actually *finish* any writing. You will sometimes need to say to them that it is time to leave a piece as it is and move on.

# Word-processing hints 4

### Age range
Six to eleven.

### Group size
Individuals or groups of three to four children.

### What you need
A computer with word-processing facility. Preferably a printer.

### What to do
When the word processor is being used heavily for children's writing, the storage and management of the various disks and tapes needed can get confusing. Disks are far more satisfactory than tapes for this purpose. They are much faster in operation and, if looked after, much more reliable. To minimise storage confusion, allot each child in the class his/her own disk for word-processing files. Clearly label the disk with the child's name, and store it centrally where the child can retrieve and replace it easily. If necessary, the files on the disk can be protected with a password known only to the individual child (and the teacher). By this means other children will not be able to spoil others' writing.

# Word processor tricks 1

### Age range
Seven to eleven.

### Group size
Group of three to four.

### What you need
A computer, preferably with a printer. A word-processing package which allows text to be moved around on the page.

### What to do
Get the children to think about a particular theme, say, 'winter', and to jot down on to the word processor screen any words or phrases which come into their heads. They do not have to make sense of them yet. When they have enough (around 15 will do for a reasonably-sized poem), they then have to assemble them, on the screen, into groups of words about the same subject. This is easily done on most word processors, using the 'cut and paste' facility. They might put all the words to do with trees in one place, all those to do with snow in another, and so on. These then form the beginnings of verses for their poem. They then try to assemble the ideas on each topic into a first draft of a verse. They will need to add linking words, and to move some words around. Once they have a first draft, they can take a hard copy of it and take it away to revise it.

# Word processor tricks 2

## Age range
Seven to eleven.

## Group size
Individuals or groups of three to four.

## What you need
A computer, preferably with a printer. A word-processing package with a 'replace' facility.

## What to do
One of the features of word processors which children immediately appreciate is the ease with which wrong spellings can be corrected. To highlight this feature, get them to start by entering text with no regard at all for spelling. If there are words which they know they cannot spell, get them to enter a short code for these words. The initial letter plus ** is very suitable. They will thus have a text similar to 1.

When they have finished writing they can then find the correct spellings of these words, in a dictionary or by asking someone. Show them how to use the 'replace' facility to change the occurences of the misspellings for correct spellings at a stroke.

Figure 1

Once upon a time there was a fierce
d**. This d** lived in a g**
cave. The d**'s cave was so g**
even the bats would not live there. The
d** had no friends.

## Follow-up
When children get proficient at this technique they might realise that it can save them a lot of writing. If they are typing in a story in which one word is used a large number of times, they can type in a brief code for it (say, ...) and then alter all these at one go at the end. This is how the author wrote the word 'word processor' in this section of this book!

# Word processor tricks 3

### Age range
Eight to eleven.

### Group size
Individuals or groups of three to four.

### What you need
A computer with word processor.

### What to do
Start with a story on the word processor of about 70 to 100 words long. Set children the task of expanding it to four times the size without adding any new events. Advise them to concentrate on descriptions both of people and of actions.

### Follow-up
It might be useful with older children to take both the initial and final story, and discuss which they think is the better. Children tend to think long stories must be better than short. This activity might provide a useful opportunity to examine this idea.

# Word processor tricks 4

### Age range
Eight to eleven.

### Group size
Individuals or groups of three to four.

### What you need
A computer with word processor.

### What to do
Start with a long story on the word processor. Set children the task of getting it to half or a third of the length without destroying the sense (of the story). Get them to think about what are the really essential parts and what are just 'frills'. They need to think about shorter ways of expressing long-winded ideas.

### Follow-up
This can be a valuable activity if later applied to their own writing. Encourage them to really think what is essential in a story.

# Word processor tricks 5

## Age range
Seven to eleven.

## Group size
Individuals or groups of three to four.

## What you need
A computer with word processor.

## What to do
Children often write stories with one or more words repeated many times. The replace facility on a word processor can be used to suggest they change this. Two common examples of this are the use of 'and' or 'and then' instead of full stops, and the use of 'nice' as the universal adjective. In the first case the teacher can use the replace facility to alter all the occurences of 'and' to something like '?.?'. In the second, every 'nice' could be altered to something like 'splodgy?'. Then send the children back to sort out their stories.

## Follow-up
With older children this technique can be used to focus attention on a whole range of stylistic effects. For example, you could alter every instance of 'very', or 'said'.

# Choosing a word processor

Choosing the right word-processing program for your children can be difficult as there is such a wide range available. The following are some considerations you might bear in mind when choosing. If at all possible, let your children try out a program before committing yourself to it.

**1** Check the facilities the program has available. There is usually a trade-off between facilities and price, but, if possible, these facilities are desirable:

- Insert and Overwrite modes;
- cut and paste;
- Search and Replace;
- control over print-out, including fonts used.

**2** Can the program be used with a Concept Keyboard? This is a flat, touch-sensitive pad, divided into squares which can be programmed to produce anything the user wishes on the screen. It can be extremely useful with younger children, as squares can be programmed with either:

- lower case letters for children confused by the upper case keyboard;
- words that the children already know, thus using the computer for a language-experience approach to reading and writing;
- words that the children may use regularly in connection with a particular topic.

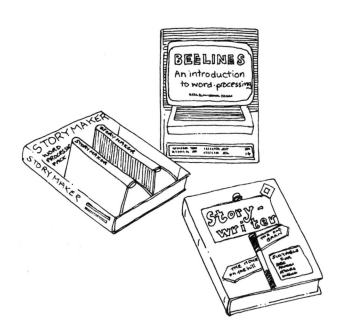

**3** Does the program have a variety of fonts available, or does it at least print on the screen in a font similar to the one used in the children's early reading books? Can it print using these fonts? This is more important for younger children, but even older children can be motivated by printing in, say, Gothic script.

**4** Is the program WYSIWYG? This is computer jargon for 'What you see is what you get', and refers to programs in which what is printed out is exactly the same as appears on the screen. Some programs do not do this, and only a few do it entirely. Do you think it matters if children can tell a program to, say, underline a line, or print some words in italics, but do not actually see the results until they get a print-out?

# Tracker books

### Age range
Seven to eleven.

### Group size
Groups of four to six children.

### What you need
Several copies of various *Choose your own adventure* books, in which the reader influences the development of the story by making decisions, and then reading the part of the story which follows on from those decisions. There are various series on sale, eg the *Fighting Fantasy Gamebooks* from Puffin.

### What to do
After letting the children read the adventure books until they are familiar with the idea of them, introduce the possibility of designing their own. They can decide on a general theme, eg *The Haunted House*, or *Lost in the Caves*. The next step is to design a flow diagram to show the routes through the book.

On the opposite page is an example of such a flow diagram. The boxes with bold outlines are pages to be written, and those with light outlines are choices to be made at the end of the pages. It may take the children several drafts before they get this to their satisfaction. When it seems to work the next step is to assign numbers to the pages. This needs care to ensure that decisions lead to the right pages and that page numbers are not used twice. When this has been arranged, the children can write the pages. They could work together on each of them, or pairs or individuals could be assigned particular pages. They will have to consult each other as they are writing to make sure that they have consistency, ie the hero/heroine needs to wear the same clothes on each page, and to look the same. When each page is written, they could perhaps be typed out and the book bound together. It will then be available for other children to read.

### Follow-up
This idea can be used with children of all junior ages, although obviously the complexity of the stories they write will vary. It can also be used with whole classes, and with pairs of children writing individual pages. In this case, consistency will need to be watched very carefully.

# LOST IN THE WOOD

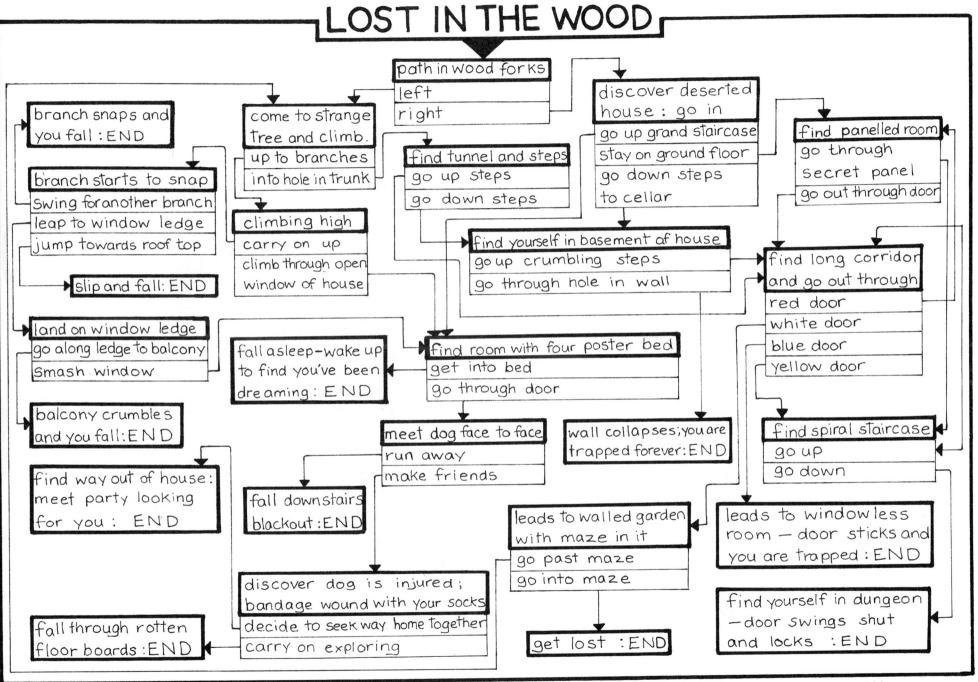

**path in wood forks**
- left
- right

**branch snaps and you fall : END**

**come to strange Tree and climb.**
- up to branches
- into hole in trunk

**discover deserted house : go in**
- go up grand staircase
- stay on ground floor
- go down steps to cellar

**find panelled room**
- go through secret panel
- go out through door

**branch starts to snap**
- Swing for another branch
- leap to window ledge
- jump towards roof top

**find tunnel and steps**
- go up steps
- go down steps

**climbing high**
- carry on up
- climb through open window of house

**Slip and fall : END**

**find yourself in basement of house**
- go up crumbling steps
- go through hole in wall

**find long corridor and go out through**
- red door
- white door
- blue door
- yellow door

**land on window ledge**
- go along ledge to balcony
- Smash window

**fall asleep – wake up to find you've been dreaming : END**

**find room with four poster bed**
- get into bed
- go through door

**balcony crumbles and you fall : END**

**meet dog face to face**
- run away
- make friends

**wall collapses; you are trapped forever : END**

**find spiral staircase**
- go up
- go down

**find way out of house: meet party looking for you : END**

**fall downstairs blackout : END**

**leads to walled garden with maze in it**
- go past maze
- go into maze

**leads to windowless room – door sticks and you are trapped : END**

**discover dog is injured; bandage wound with your socks**
- decide to seek way home together
- carry on exploring

**find yourself in dungeon – door swings shut and locks : END**

**fall through rotten floor boards : END**

**get lost : END**

# Computerised trackers 1

### Age range
Six to eleven.

### Group size
Groups of four to six children.

### What you need
A computer, ideally with a printer. Software designed to allow the construction of 'interactive stories'.

### What to do
There are several computer programs available which facilitate the writing of stories where the reader determines the development of the plot (see Tracker Books page 108). For the BBC computer, TRACKS is available as part of the M.E.P. Language Development pack, STORYWRITER is available from E.S.M. These packs are largely self-explanatory, but it should be noted that the stories that children create using them should be largely designed before the computer is actually used. This means that flow diagrams will need to be drafted, as with the previous idea, although with simpler stories these will not need to be as complex.

Children 'read' the stories, individually or preferably in small groups, on the computer screen, although the software usually allows them to print out the story they read if a printer is available.

### Follow-up
If you have a printer, the children's stories could be printed out and then assembled into 'Choose your own adventure' stories. This will allow the children to use them when the computer is not available.

# Computerised trackers 2

## Age range
Seven to eleven.

## Group size
Whole class or groups of four to six.

## What you need
A computer. A teletext-emulator program such as EDFAX, or MICRO-VIEWDATA.

## What to do
You can design an interactive adventure story using software which allows the computer to emulate teletext. Many children will be familiar with teletext from using CEEFAX or ORACLE at home, but even those that are not will quickly get the hang of it. Plan the story using a flow diagram as previously explained. Each page will need to be designed as a frame. In EDFAX, it is possible to link frames together so that readers will not need to choose after each frame. When a choice is necessary, readers choose which page to go to next by entering a three-figure number. The program itself deals with this so all children have to do is actually design each frame of the story, and ensure that readers are given clear information on which numbers to key in.

## Follow-up
One of the advantages of this system of designing interactive stories over the previous one, is the easy inclusion of graphics in each page of the story. Children quickly learn how to design their own pictures using a program like EDFAX, and these can be incorporated into their stories.

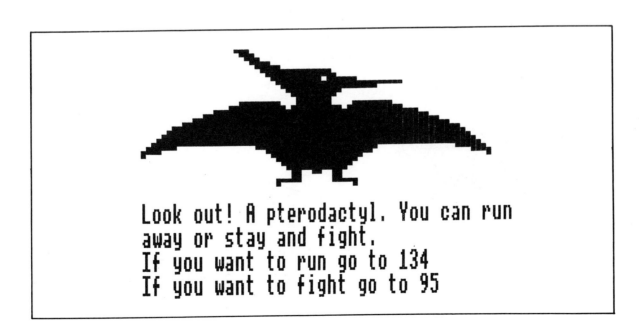

Look out! A pterodactyl. You can run away or stay and fight.
If you want to run go to 134
If you want to fight go to 95

# Computerised magazines

## Age range
Seven to eleven.

## Group size
Groups of four to six.

## What you need
A computer. A teletext-emulator program such as EDFAX, or MICRO-VIEWDATA.

## What to do
Children can use teletext-emulator programs to design their own screen-based magazines. Pages can incorporate text, graphics of various kinds, and sometimes can have messages hidden on them which readers can reveal by pressing a certain key (good for joke punchlines, and quiz answers). It will usually be found that once they have been shown the possiblities and allowed to experiment, children rapidly become much more competent at designing pages than their teachers. The key to this work, then, is to give them plenty of opportunity for experimenting.

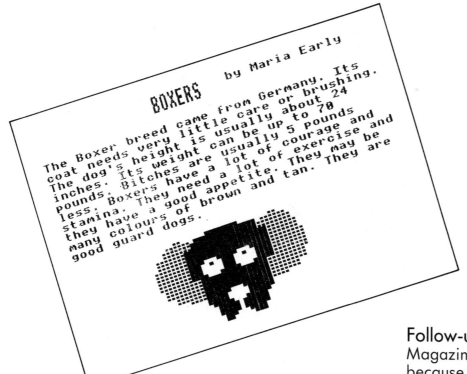

## Follow-up
Magazines designed this way have a useful spin-off because a computer can be set automatically to run them at such events as parents' evenings etc. This gives a novel and entertaining way of displaying children's work.

# Computerised newspapers

## Age range
Seven to eleven.

## Group size
Whole class or groups of four to six.

## What you need
A computer and a printer. Software designed to help with the production of newspaper-style pages. The simplest of these packages is probably FRONT PAGE EXTRA, distributed free to its members by M.A.P.E. More complex are the 'publishing' packages such as FLEET STREET EDITOR and PAGEMAKER.

## What to do
Use of these packages is largely self-explanatory, although they clearly vary widely in complexity and ease of use. Lower junior children will have little trouble with FRONT PAGE, but the full-blown publishing packages will be found difficult to use, although feasible with help, by top juniors.

Get children to roughly plan the layout of the pages they will produce before using the computer. They need to decide the balance of text to graphics (in FRONT PAGE children simply leave gaps for pictures, which are drawn or stuck in afterwards), and the headlines and sub-headings they will use. Newspaper pages can be designed as general news carriers or to report on more specific things like class visits etc (see figure 1).

**VICTORIA TIMES**

8th October 1986

10p

# WE VISIT THE FARM

All the children thought we had a lovely day, and Mrs. Simpson, our teacher, agreed.

**A strange pig**

The funniest part of the day was when we visited the pig pen. There was a pig called Charlie there and he was very funny. He kept running around his pen and squealing, "Oink, Oink". We tried to feed him all our sandwiches, that he liked him all her lunch and then she was hungry later. Mrs. Simpson said it was her own fault, but then she gave Joanne some of her lunch.

Oink Oink

**A lovely day**

Yesterday Class Two went on a visit to Hall Street farm. We were there to study how some of the animals lived.

Get your eggs at Hall Street farm

Figure 1

---

Figure 2

**SCIENCE NEWS**

000

---

# EXPERIMENTS WITH AIR

**The egg in the bottle trick**

Do you know how to get a hard boiled egg inside a milk bottle?

**What you need**

You need a milk bottle, a hard boiled egg without the shell, and a bowl of very hot water.

**What you do**

Stand the bottle in the hot water for at least ten minutes. When it is very hot place the egg on the neck of the bottle. Take the bottle out of the hot water and stand it in some cold water. Watch what happens.

**Why does this work?**

Can you explain what has happened? How could you get the egg out again?

eggs can be magic

## Follow-up

Using these packages it is possible for children to produce work sheets on special topics for other members of the class. This might be as simple as adding a few questions to the bottom of a page, or it might be made more complex (see figure 2).

# Reproducible material

# Teaching hand writing 1, see page 30

Begin at ●, follow the arrows

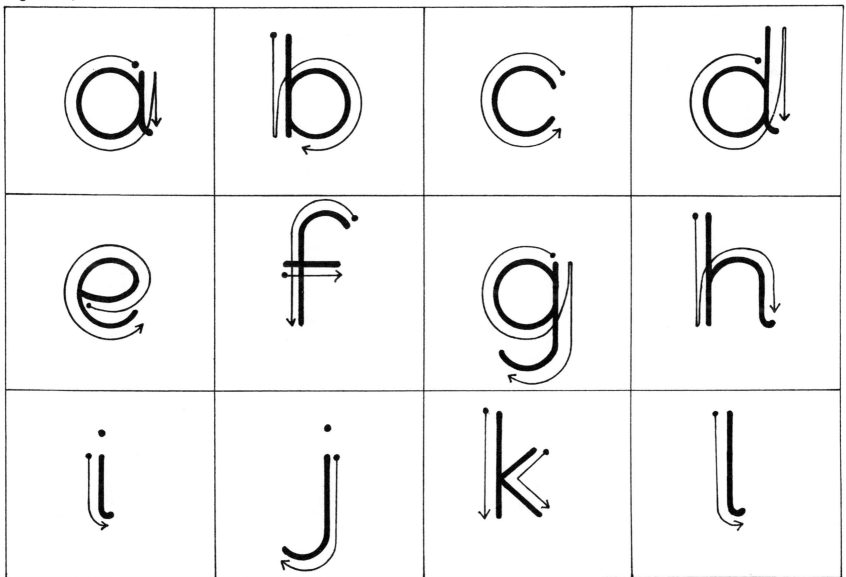

# Teaching hand writing 1, see page 30

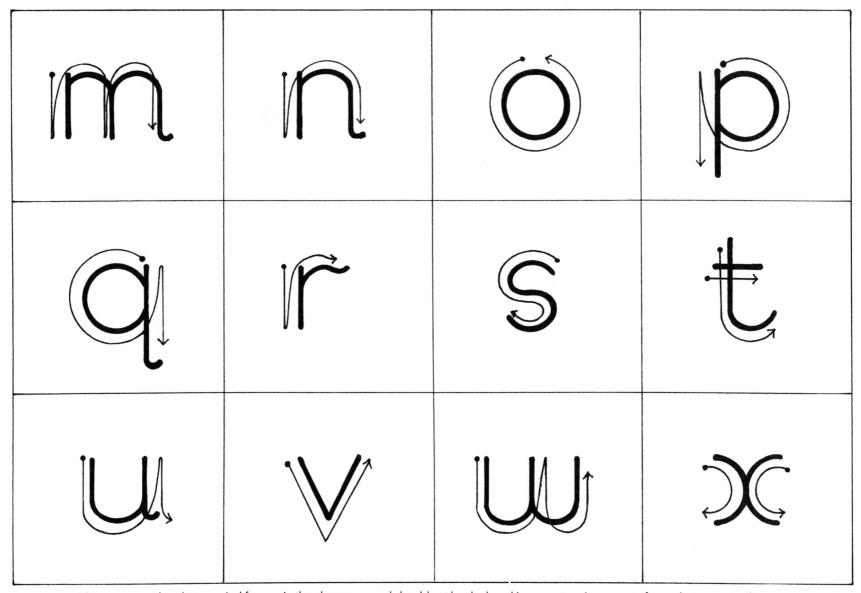

# Teaching hand writing 1, see page 30

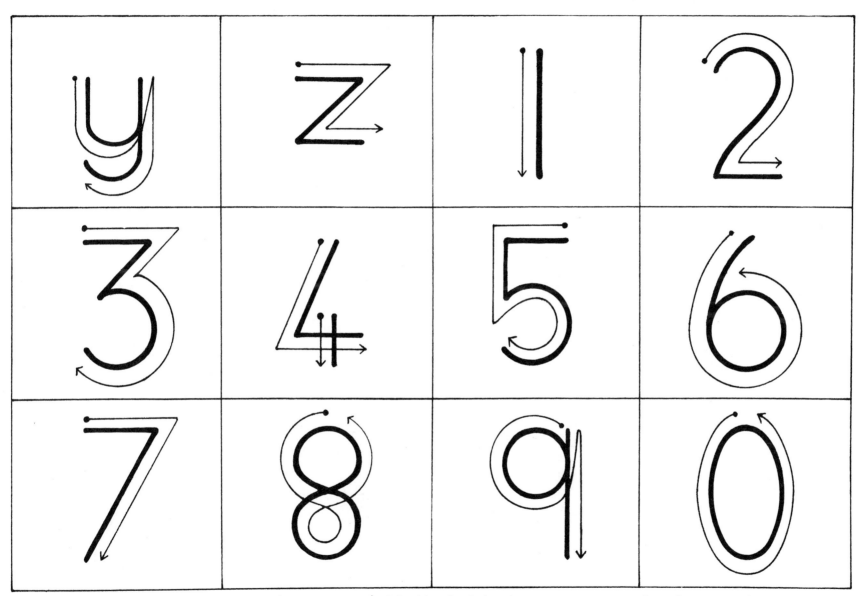

# Story wheel, see page 73

Cut out each wheel. Assemble them together with a paper fastener.

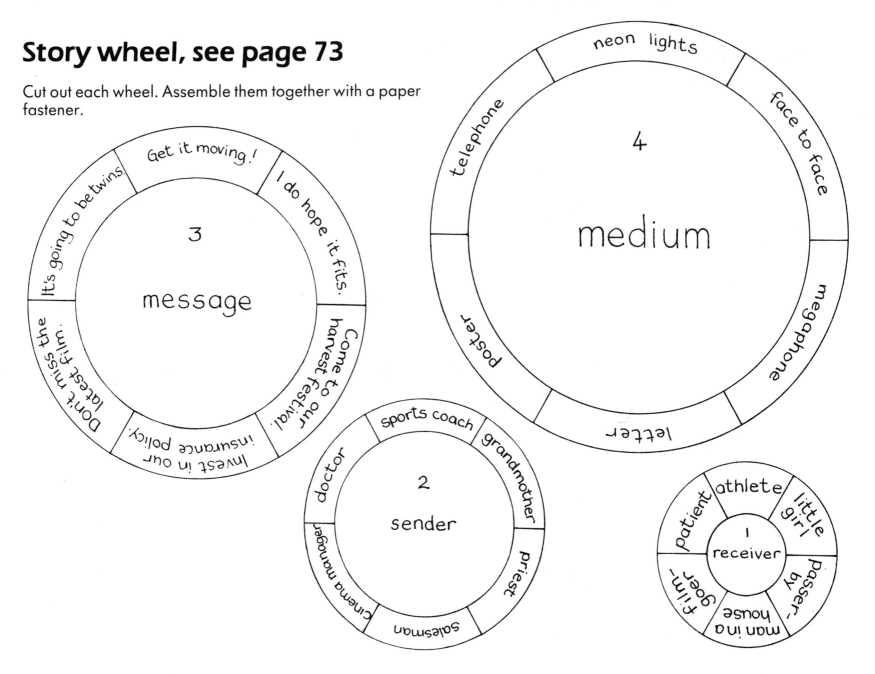

# Make-a-story chart, see page 73

Start with the 'person' box and follow one of the arrows to another box. Then choose another arrow and move to another box – and so on. Write down the words from the boxes you choose – do they help you to think of a story?

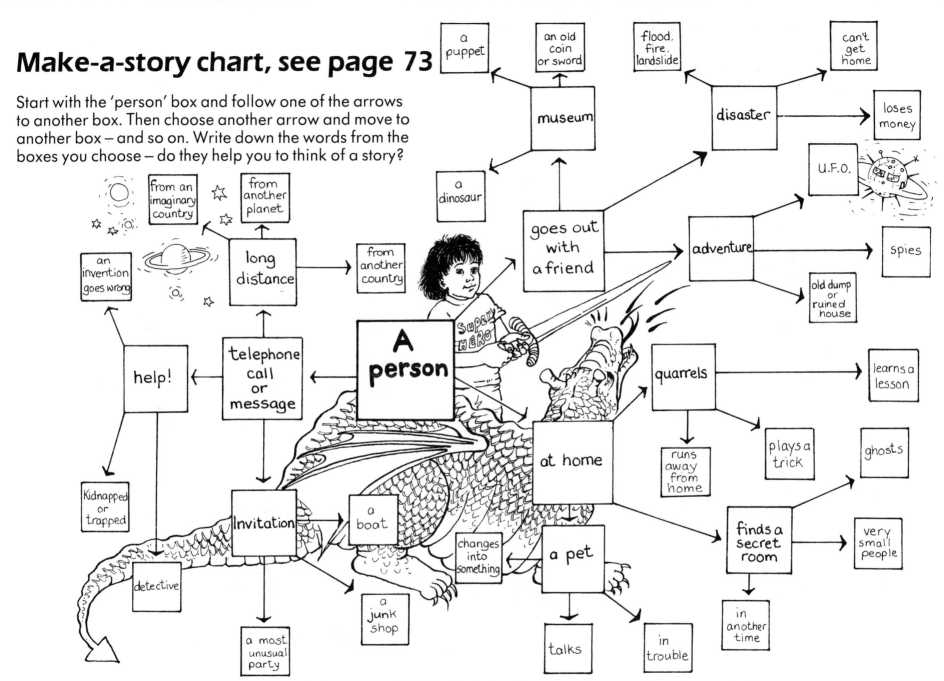

- a puppet
- an old coin or sword
- flood, fire, landslide
- can't get home
- museum
- disaster
- loses money
- U.F.O.
- a dinosaur
- goes out with a friend
- adventure
- spies
- from an imaginary country
- from another planet
- old dump or ruined house
- an invention goes wrong
- long distance
- from another country
- help!
- telephone call or message
- A person
- quarrels
- learns a lesson
- at home
- plays a trick
- ghosts
- Kidnapped or trapped
- runs away from home
- detective
- Invitation
- a boat
- changes into something
- a pet
- finds a secret room
- very small people
- a junk shop
- a most unusual party
- talks
- in trouble
- in another time

In the next few pages 'Good Morning' is written in some of the languages of the world.

Punjabi

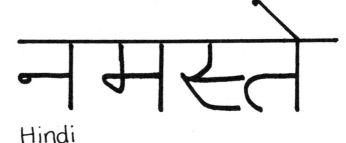

Hindi

Bengali

# A celebration of writing, see page 11

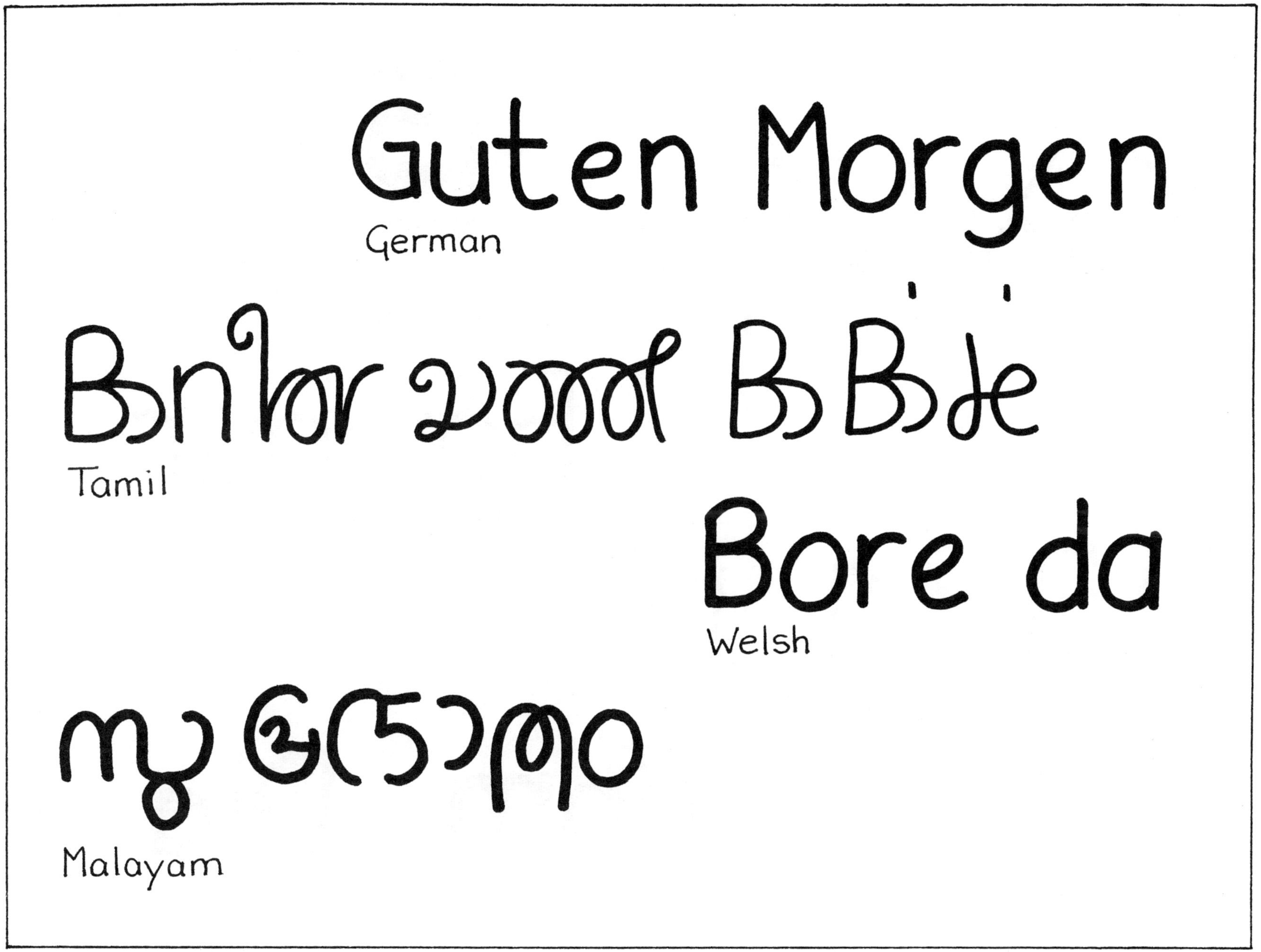
Guten Morgen
German
Tamil
Bore da
Welsh
Malayam

Καλη μέρα
Greek

早晨
Cantonese

Bonjour
French

Urdu

Bom Dia
Portuguese

# Further reading

*Children's Writing in the Primary School*, R Beard, Hodder & Stoughton (1984)

*Writing: Teachers and Children at Work*, D Graves, Heinemann (1983)

*A Researcher Learns to Write*, D Graves, Heinemann (1984)

*Making Language Work*, D Hutchcroft, McGraw-Hill (1981)

*Creative Writing*, S Marshall, MacMillan (1974)

'The use of the word processor with developing writers – helping children think about writing' by B Smith in *Micro-Explorations (2)* eds D Wray and F Potter, UKRA (1986)

*Teaching Writing: The Development of Written Language Skills*, G Thornton, Edward Arnold (1980)

'Primary observations of word processing' by J Trushell and C Broderick in *Micro-Explorations (1)* eds D Wray and F Potter, UKRA (1984)

'Drafting in the classroom' by D Wray and J Gallimore in *Primary Teaching Studies* (Vol 1, No 3, June 1986)

# Acknowlegements

The editors and publishers extend grateful thanks for the reuse of material first published in *Junior Education* and *Child Education* to: Andrew Bryden for 'Binding your own books' and 'Covering your own books'; Bill Michael for 'Ready to write' and 'Teaching handwriting 1'; Frank Flynn for 'Collaborative story writing' and 'Structural poetry'; Judith Nicholls for 'A marathon write' and 'Acrostic introductions'; Fay Howat for 'Using the story wheel' and 'Using the story chart'; Cliff Moon for 'The word bank', 'Try it again sheets' and 'Speech marks'; Clive Butler for 'Tracker books'; Irene Yates for 'Illustrating metaphors'.

Every effort has been made to trace and acknowledge contributions. If any right has been omitted, the publishers offer their apologies and will rectify this in subsequent editions following notification.

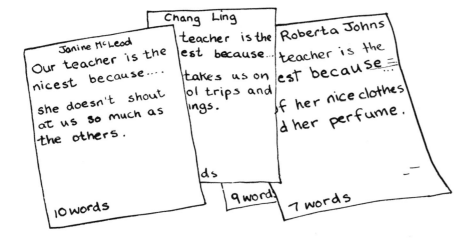

# Other Scholastic books

## Bright Ideas

The *Bright Ideas* books provide a wealth of resources for busy primary school teachers. There are now more than 20 titles published, providing clearly explained and illustrated ideas on topics ranging from *Writing* and *Maths Activities* to *Assemblies* and *Christmas Art and Craft*. Each book contains material which can be photocopied for use in the classroom.

## Teacher Handbooks

The *Teacher Handbooks* give an overview of the latest research in primary education, and show how it can be put into practice in the classroom. Covering all the core areas of the curriculum, the *Teacher Handbooks* are indispensable to the new teacher as a source of information and useful to the experienced teacher as a quick reference guide.

## Management Books

The *Management Books* are designed to help teachers to organise their time, classroom and teaching more efficiently. The books deal with topical issues, such as *Parents and Schools* and organising and planning *Project Teaching*, and are written by authors with lots of practical advice and experiences to share.

## Let's Investigate

*Let's Investigate* is an exciting range of photocopiable maths activity books giving open-ended investigative tasks. The series will complement and extend any existing maths programme. Designed to cover the 6 to 12-year-old age range these books are ideal for small group or individual work. Each book presents progressively more difficult concepts and many of the activities can be adapted for use throughout the primary school. Detailed teacher's notes outlining the objectives of each photocopiable sheet and suggesting follow-up activities have been included.